FINDING THE FUN AGAIN!

Recharging

Your

Relationship

JACK MUMEY AND CYNTHIA TINSLEY

Fairview Press
Minneapolis

This book is for Jennifer and Ernie. This couple is marvelous, recharging, and so exemplary of friendship that we cannot do them justice. They do all this stuff (well, most) mentioned in this book. They recharge, and they apply everything to their lives and their other relationships. They inspire us to believe that what we have to say is possible for others, and not just a fluke of our imaginations.

Published by Fairview Press, 2450 Riverside Avenue South, Minneapolis, MN 55454

Library of Congress Cataloging-in-Publication Data

Mumey, Jack
Recharging your relationship / Jack Mumey and Cynthia Tinsley.
          p.   cm.
At head of title: : Finding the fun again
ISBN 0-925190-34-9 (alk. paper) : $10.95
1. Married people--United States--Psychology.   2.   Interpersonal   relations--United States.   3. Communication in marriage--United States.   I.   Tinsley, Cynthia. II. Title.
HQ734.M883   1995
646.7'8--dc20   94-47468
                                                                          CIP

First Printing: January 1995

Printed in the United States of America
99   98   97   96   95   7   6   5   4   3   2   1

Cover design: Nancekivell Group

Publisher's Note: Fairview Press publishes books and other materials related to the subjects of physical health, mental health, chemical dependency, and other family issues. Its publications, including *Recharging Your Relationship* do not necessarily reflect the philosophy of Fairview Hospital and Healthcare Services or their treatment programs.

The paper used in this publication meets the minimum requirements of American National Standard for Information Sciences—Permanence of Paper for Printed Library Materials, ANSI Z329.48-1984.

Contents

Acknowledgments

We are blessed indeed to have Ed Wedman, publisher of Fairview Press, as a champion of our projects from the beginning. Nearing the end of this project, we lost our senior editor, Jack Caravela, who branched out on his own. We are so happy for him that he is doing what he wants. We thank him, we miss him, and we wish him good luck!

Our new editor, Jay Hanson, has brought a fresh insight into our work and has not been afraid to practice a little recharging himself! Jay has been especially helpful in the area of parenting as related to the topics of this book.

Our families—scattered between Denver, Lubbock, Plantation, and Phoenix—maintain a decided influence on us. We are not only grateful for their support but are profoundly aware of their contribution to our writing and our lives. So we tip our hats to Jack's children—Jackson (Florida), Tracey, Dana, and Dawn (Colorado); Cyn's folks Jim and Dean, Nancy and Duane, and Laurene (Texas); and her sister Kim and brother-in-law Ron (Arizona). We know that without their encouragement and their offers to let us hang out with them a few days a year, we're sure nothing quite as productive as this book would happen.

We are not so sure that the people in our lives whom we acknowledge really comprehend their contribution to this product and other projects we tackle. This book might have been written by someone else eventually. It was written this way, by Jack and Cyn, at this time, for all these many reasons, because all of the people we mention did what they did and were put here to do. Part of what they're here to do is help us write. We take credit for putting the message into words. They all get credit for the feelings that needed words.

Oh, by the way. Any mistakes or absolutely off-the-wall and totally unworkable ideas in this book are strictly the fault of the coauthor. (Um, the coauthor just declared herself author. Funny how he put that part in just now.)

Jack Mumey and Cynthia Tinsley

Introduction

Ｗe work hard at recharging our relationship. We do it on a daily basis. We don't mean just once or twice a day, but all day every day. When the stresses of our professional lives make us "gritchy" at one another, it is not uncommon for us to plan a "Ten-Minute Drill" (see page 81) for in the morning, the afternoon, and the evening if necessary.

When writing deadlines come closer, so do the drill times. We are happy to charge a lot of that connection to being coauthors and husband and wife. We also notice a similar correspondence under any kind of pressure. This happens. We're coming ever closer to knowing that and accepting it, and that's part of what we want to share in this book. To paraphrase a rather popular bumper sticker, "stuff" happens. When we know and accept stuff happens, then we can focus on our partners and their needs rather than on the stuff. Stuff will always be there—it's a fact of life.

The idea for this book came from Jack's psychotherapy practice, more than fifteen years in successful existence. But the practical applications of exactly how couples could recharge came from Cyn's insistence that "we ought to be practicing what you preach." (Cyn would note here that she also had some ideas that were totally unrelated to Jack's practice and seem to have some practical application.)

The AIDS crisis, the complexity of family life, the strains of meeting and courting, single parenthood, to name only a few relationship challenges, make us (as Hamlet said) "rather bear those ills we have, than fly to others that we know not of." In other words, why not put your energies as a couple—your synergies—into building a renewed, stronger existing relationship?

It is considerably better to get a couple in sync with each other than to "shoot a whole new film." As we looked around at couples we observed, it became more clear to us that our efforts to recharge what we have with each other were paying off.

Even today we look at other couples in restaurants or at concerts, plays, or sports events, and we can identify a couple who could be on the cutting edge of recharging. So what keeps them from doing it? Plainly, fear. The specter of change that causes fear will keep many couples from improving their relationship. It will keep them tied into old ways, old habits, and old (very old) relationships.

We hope you will accept the challenges we provide in this book. We are confident that you can find new life in a relationship and new ways to balance a relationship. There are newer ideas to hook up the emotional battery cables and hook up to recharge your partner (and you), breathe new life into a complex set of behaviors that we call "relationships," and find great rewards for your efforts.

By the way, we would love to receive any comments about this book or your efforts at recharging your relationship that are different from ours. Any comments at all will be carefully reviewed and taken to heart, we promise. (Cyn says we won't just review them, we'll probably try them.) Write us:

CynJac Communications
3140-K So. Peoria St. Suite 430
Aurora, CO 80014

1 Recharge? Passion? Are You Kidding?

Y ou are sitting in your favorite chair, watching television or reading. You look at the person sharing your space and life, and you wonder who that person is. When did you begin not to know her? When did he become a stranger?

Maybe the love of your life does something very strange. (Eating raw Spam sandwiches with bell pepper and peanut butter qualifies here.) You find yourself wondering how you could have been so foolishly blind. Perhaps you even feel a little queasy and shaky. Who knows if there are even more strange behaviors that the future may reveal?

Relationships are complicated and bewildering, mysterious and confusing. So much so that many people give up trying to have them work. Or they pretend to try but don't really do anything. Or they simply allow the relationship to happen almost as if they had no influence over it.

We've got some good news and some bad news for you. Relationships are hard work, recharging them even harder. The

1

good news is the joy of the process of actively recharging your relationship and keeping it charged far outweighs the work involved. In fact, the work of recharging can actually be a lot of fun. The bad news? That work can also be very personally challenging, as is all work that leads to growth and change.

You may be thinking that your relationship is fine. You don't really need to work on it or recharge it. Our intent is not to suggest your relationship needs first aid, although some readers may have chosen this book hoping for a bandage.

Our intent in *Recharging Your Relationship*, rather, is to suggest the possibility of taking a good relationship and making it great. Even better, you can take a great relationship and make it out of sight. We also know some relationships are better left—we're sorry that there is no better way to say that. You can use the exercises and suggestions in the Passion Points sections at the end of each chapter regardless of the state of your relationship. They can help you clarify what you want to recharge.

Recharging a relationship includes not only activity, but also mental exercise. The way you perceive your relationship and your partner is very important. As with most important issues, there are at least two ways to look at a relationship. You can focus on the positive aspects, or you can focus on the negative aspects. In that choice of focus lies the true source of your power to create an extraordinary relationship.

The process is like that of a man married to a completely plain, perhaps even unattractive, woman. However, he believes with all his heart she is the most beautiful woman on the planet. He constantly thinks of her as beautiful and praises her beauty. She begins over time to believe she is indeed beautiful, and carries herself as if she is. Ultimately, she becomes beautiful to all who see her by virtue of her belief in the man who believes in her.

We challenge you to exercise your perception muscle. If you can imagine just how exciting, surprising, and empowering your relationship can be, this book is for you. We want to take you (and ourselves as we exercise with you) into the possibilities for your relationship beyond imagination.

"But," you ask, "what if my partner won't or can't do the same?" First of all, do this for yourself. Consider that if you perceive your partner as beautiful, then you at the very least will be fortunate enough to have a beautiful partner. At best, you may find your commitment to recharging your relationship inspires your partner.

Some possible ideas, however, for helping your partner become interested in recharging include activities or reminders from the early days of your romance. For example, you might play music you listened to when you were first dating. You could go someplace or recreate a setting that reminds you of some of your first times together or when you first realized you loved each other. Think of some of the foods or aromas that remind you and your partner of your first dates. You may have to use all of these ideas and more of your own over a period of time to spark your partner's desire to recharge your relationship, but it's definitely worth a try.

Julia Sugarbaker, a character in the television series *Designing Women*, had a line in one episode that struck Cyn's fancy. "Life is like a dog sled team," Julia said. "If you ain't the lead dog, the scenery never changes." This statement vividly expresses a reason to take the lead.

In the following pages we will address some of the more important issues involved in relationship. Our Passion Points at the end of each chapter will offer ideas and exercises to help you recharge your relationship. We hope you will try them all. Because we are talking about change, which can be uncomfortable, we encourage you to at least work with the most comfortable ideas or exercises at first. Later you can come back to those more challenging for you.

Now, to find the fun again!

Passion Points

1. **Perception Power Stretch.** Look around your home or office, and notice items you use for a purpose other than that for which they were designed. For example, a coffee mug used as a pencil holder. Next, look at different items and try to think of at least three other uses for each of them. For example, a wooden chair could be used as a writing table if you sit on the floor. It could also be used as an exercise bench while doing leg lifts or as a plant stand.

    Once you've thought of other uses for a particular object, notice if your perception of that object has changed. Do you still see merely a chair, or have you begun to see it as a representation of possibilities?

2. **Attraction Flex.** Take a moment to jot down five characteristics that initially attracted you to your partner. Do this quickly - write the first five traits that come to mind.

3. **Memory Extension.** Take a few more minutes just before going to sleep or just after waking to remember how you felt about your partner when you first got together.

4. **Perception Crunches.** In one column write three of your part-ner's behaviors that irritate you. In a second column next to each irritating behavior write a positive aspect of that behavior that benefits you. For example:

    *   *Eats disgusting sandwiches*   I don't have to eat them.
    *   *Turns the TV up too loud*   I can practice my
                                       concentration skills.

    *   *Makes me feel stupid*   I can learn to think
                                       well of myself despite what
                                       others think.

5. **Cooling Down.** Tear up anything you've written if you are at all concerned about anyone else finding your notes.

2 Dumping the Past

So who cares? Your relationship (even if it is the only one you've had) has so many bad memories, so many problems. Who has the energy to try to recharge? In fact, do you even care about the relationship anymore?

So who cares? We do, and really, way down deep inside, so do you. After all, you began a relationship because you believed it would be something different. Notice we say relationship rather than marriage or any other descriptive word or phrase that denotes two people cohabitating together. The reason for this is we want to deal with the relationship part of two people's lives. A marriage or a living arrangement could be compared to computer hardware. The shell remains essentially the same. A relationship, however, is like the software. It runs the computer, tells the hardware what to do and how to perform. Software requires attention. Old files have to be deleted periodically, software upgrades are necessary to meet the changing needs of the user, new programs have to be integrated with the old. The hardware is useless without the software, and the quality of the software determines the quality of the computer's output. So it is with a marriage and a relationship. The two can be separate, but the true quality is determined by the quality of the relationship when the two are integrated.

It's pointless, then, to work on your marriage or living arrangement. You already have one of those, for better or for worse as the traditional phrasing goes. What you don't have is a relationship. Get mad at us, but it may be true. Stop and think about the last time the two of you had a real date, for instance. Or, can you easily recall when you shared a moment or two of hugging and kissing without sex? In fact, how long has it been since the "hug store" was open for business? Even if your criteria for a rewarding, fulfilling relationship are different, chances are that more of those criteria can be met.

Lose the Baggage

An obstacle in this search for a relationship worthy of recharging is old baggage from the past. This baggage consists of memories and behaviors earlier in your current relationship or in previous ones. Like all baggage, it can be so heavy that it drains all your energy to carry it, along with all your desire to even try hooking up emotional battery cables for a recharge.

How did this happen? How did you manage to drag all those old trunks full of anger, mistrust, shame, guilt, and . . . well, you put the tags on the trunks. You know better than we do what makes up emotional baggage from your past. What it all amounts to is you looking at your own image in the mirror for the umpteenth time and asking, "How can I let go? How can I get rid of the baggage from the past?"

Good questions, and we're glad you asked. For you to recharge your relationship it is absolutely vital that you drag all those old trunks out to the curb and dump them.

Think of Jacob Marley, the long dead partner of Ebenezer Scrooge in the classic *A Christmas Carol*. When Marley's ghost first confronts the miserly Scrooge, he is fettered. The links of the chains are so enormous and heavy that he has difficulty dragging them across the floor to confront the skeptical Scrooge. With a little literary license, the scene goes something like this:

"Tell me, Jacob, why are you chained?" asks Scrooge.

"This is the chain I forged in life. I forged it link by link, yard by yard, and I daresay yours was as heavy and long as this seven Christmas Eves ago!" wails the ghost.

Baggage. Garbage. Emotional leftovers that have hardened into a chain around your ability to function well in a relationship. It doesn't matter what kind of a relationship you are in—married, heterosexual, gay or lesbian, racially mixed, ethnically mixed. If you are one of two people engaged in an emotional, physical, and psychological bonding process over a period of time, then you are in a relationship.

Even newlyweds find the joy of the wedding can slip away very quickly, if allowed to do so. Often the culprit for allowing this to happen much sooner than anticipated is that emotional baggage from your past. That baggage can get in the way big time and can seem like elephant dung on a new white shag carpet.

Why Lose the Baggage?

What triggers this old stuff? What springs open the locks on those old steamer trunks and allows all the old troubles to come pouring out, smothering you and what you have going for you now? Some of the keys are the actions and reactions of the person with whom you are involved today. Your partner does or says something, or acts or looks, like someone in your past. We'll call this phenomenon the "Mistaken Partner Identification."

We'll use an example of excessive drinking to illustrate. Let's say your last relationship involved the awful nightmare of alcoholism. You managed to free yourself from that situation, and now you are in a relationship that seems perfect. Then one night at a party, your current partner drinks a little too much. Oh, boy.

Suddenly, you find yourself reacting as you did to your previous alcoholic partner's behavior. You expect the worst as a result of your partner's overindulgence. The old chains you forged of anger, codependence, enabling, shame, hurt, fear—all that stuff—snake out of your old steamer trunks. They seem to coil around your body, constricting your breathing and weighing you down.

The poor person you are with is not an alcoholic but exhibits just enough bad behavior to trigger those old feelings. You dump on yourself and very likely your partner, too. That's old baggage. You have to recognize it for what it is and remember this is a different person who (in this example) may simply have had too much to drink. He may be acting like that other person temporarily. The problem is that you treat him just like you treated your former partner. Your relationship gets stuck for the moment, maybe longer, because you don't let go of the past experiences. Instead, you bring them forward into the present situation.

Recharging your present relationship can't take place unless you rid yourself of yesterday's baggage and approach today as if you were a newborn baby with no history. A good first step is to talk to your partner about what he or she did that started this downward slide into yesterday's garbage dump.

"Boy, you really had me going there for awhile," you say rather bravely. "It was like I was back with Chuck when I saw how you were weaving around the room at the party." Confess that you were confused about your partner's identity for awhile and that your own emotions were out of control.

Dumping the past may be more difficult if there is a payoff for you in holding on to yesterday's baggage. We know that may sound weird—a payoff to holding on to old baggage? Maybe there is some reward you find in not moving on with your relationship. Maybe you really like being a martyr, or maybe pouting is what you do best these days. If holding onto the old stuff from the past helps you stay in a pouting mood, then we guess you won't move on.

A Tool to Help

A tool we use as a couple is to ask one another, "Are we through with this hurt yet?" Or, "Can we let go of this and move on now?" If one or the other partner is not ready to move on, then we need to talk some more and that's what we do.

The first few minutes after you agree to let the issue go and move on are usually awkward. A few minutes before, she was actively searching for the iron skillet to test on his skull, and he was actively considering shattering all the china on her head. Suddenly being nice to each other can be a strain. Stick with it. It won't be long before you forget to think about what you were arguing over. Usually, if you're really committed to moving on, within a day or two you'll be kidding each other about whatever the issue was.

We always try to nail down the particular behavior that caused one of us to drag out the old baggage, then find a way to promise to change that behavior. Cyn is a great one for urging one or both of us to take a look at that particular behavior in ourselves. Jack, ever the therapist, is inclined to rifle through his extensive case histories and relate to those instead of looking at the current situation. Cyn might try to justify her current behavior based on her past experiences in another relationship. Fortunately, we both use the tools well. We keep on talking through the issue until we arrive at a way to dump the old baggage and really do change the behavior that brought it up in the first place.

Being human, sometimes it's not easy for one or both of us to move on immediately. In those cases, Cyn usually says, "Okay, fifteen minutes sulking time, starting now."

Putting the fun back into a situation where you have committed "Mistaken Partner Identification" is a challenge. "For one awful minute you looked a little bit like Chuck," she might say, playfully.

"Well, for a minute there, the way you were acting, I kinda felt like Chuck," he might respond, just as playfully. Or, she may say, "You know when you did that (the offending behavior), I was so happy to realize that you really have tried to not do that as much.

You get a gold star on your chart!"

We knew a couple, Jen and Ken, in their second marriage who were constantly calling each other by names we didn't recognize. They were not the names of either ex-partner. Our curiosity got the better of us one evening when we were playing cards together. "What's this Sally and Rob business?" we asked.

"Oh, those are names we selected based on All In The Family. You know, the old TV show? Sally Struthers and Rob Reiner played Archie's daughter and her husband who Archie was always calling 'Meathead,' " she told us. "When we start doing some dumb thing now and then, we start calling each other 'Sally' or 'Rob' because we tend to act exactly like they did in that show."

"You have to admit it breaks up the tension between us,"Ken said. "We used to get into some serious fights until we just happened on this gimmick. I think I hollered at Jen something like, 'God, are you trying to be a dumb blonde like Sally whats-her-name?' "

Jen replied, "I said Sally's last name that Ken couldn't remember, adding, 'How's that for dumb-blonde memory, Meathead?' "

Ken continued, "I shouted back 'Oh yeah, well the name's Rob if you're gonna be Sally!' I know we both started laughing so hard that it's stuck with us ever since. It's a great tension breaker between us."

Now that's putting fun back into a relationship!

Fair Fighting

Couples will fight. The idea is to fight fairly and to deal with the existing present-day issue, not the old stuff from the past. In the Passion Points at the end of this chapter, we'll give you the rules of fair fighting so you can keep them handy when you and your partner get into it.

Another point about emotional baggage is that clinging to it creates mental clutter in the present. Ask yourself if your inability to let go might be grounded in reluctance to admit failure. An entire relationship can fail, or there can be a period of failure when the relationship has been devoid of warmth, love, sex, friendship, and other qualities of intimacy. If you keep resurrecting the old baggage, you won't have to admit you had any part at all in the failure of all or part of the relationship.

You can always claim the failure was her fault or his fault. Therefore, you remain innocent, in your own mind, of any blame. You are afraid to move on and can always find many good reasons to live in the past, just to prove what a terrific effort you made and how he or she was the bad apple in the relationship.

The more you play that scenario, the better you look in it. Then you become self-righteous and begin playing the old tapes that intensify your position as the number-one historical martyr. Well, hysterical martyr might be a better tag to put on yourself.

We suggest the longer you linger in this old trash pile, the less you allow your current relationship a new charge. Letting go of the baggage is called growth.

Growing within a relationship is the most rewarding experience a couple can share. Growth means new life. It means the opportunity to expand the world in which the two of you live and to break out of those binding chains forged in the past.

Take Your Emotional Temperature

We take our emotional temperature on a regular basis by asking, "Do you still love me?" This seems an obvious question after two people have quarrelled. What about when there has been no quarrel? Then the question, "Do you still love me?" calls for an imaginative answer such as, "Of course! How can you even wonder?" Or you can ask, "How do you feel about me?" Another good question is, "Are we doing okay?" (A wise response is an immediate one. The impact is lost if you take time to think about your answer.) We suggest you ask one of these questions, or similar questions, at least once each day.

No, this isn't silly or foolish. It is a way to connect the recharging cables of the relationship and deliver a little boost without much effort. These questions allow you to reinforce the joy of your relationship and bring up any issues standing in the way of total joy.

We focused on developing this reassuring love exchange as a way of keeping in touch with our feelings about each other. We had discussed some of our previous relationships in which we didn't have a clue about the other person's feelings. So we began to measure our emotional temperature often as a fun, hands-off method of communicating. We've included an exercise in the Passion Points which expands on this process.

What makes the "hands-off" aspect of these exchanges important? We, like many other couples, don't have a lot of time together. So one advantage of separating the emotional and physical contact is we can express love regardless of our activities or locations. A second advantage is the clarity of the expression of love. Hands-off means there is no confusion about whether you love or are loved for yourself, or whether the expression of love is a disguised request for sex.

If you think we are simply a couple of insecure neurotics, you're wrong. This simple but meaningful exchange is a way we use to let go of old behaviors from the past when we were unsure of the other person's feelings. Such an exchange on a frequent basis clearly helps us dump some of our emotional baggage. You can develop similar tools to help you part with your old baggage.

Sharing Your Baggage

An important benefit of sharing your old baggage with your partner is that doing so allows each of you to be considerate of the other's triggers. True, you share what are essentially vulnerabilities. You also give your partner a gift, which is your trust that he or she won't take advantage of your soft spots.

We knew a couple who were married to each other for four years and both were in a second marriage. We were startled more than once to hear them call each other by the names of their previous mates, particularly when they were squabbling with one another.

Sensing this practice could be more destructive than positive, we confronted them about their behavior during dinner one evening.

"Well, when Carrie says something dumb like that, she might as well be Helen," said our friend, Merrill.

"And you know what? He pisses me off when he starts calling me Helen. I just throw Tim's name (her ex-husband) back at him," Carrie seethed.

"What does that accomplish?" we wondered. "Particularly since the two of you don't seem to solve the problem, but just resort to name calling."

Carrie said, "That's the point. It doesn't solve anything, but it sure lets the steam off."

We don't find that behavior healthy at all. In fair fighting, avoid name calling at all costs. We told our friends that and asked them to concentrate on the issue and free their previous mates from participation, even if only by name. The difference between this exchange between Merrill and Carrie and the one between Jen and Ken mentioned earlier is in the intent. Jen and Ken used humor and names of fictional characters to diffuse their anger. Merrill and Carrie used names of real people about whom they had a lot of emotional charge. Their intent was to goad each other and elevate the level of anger.

Dumping the past and letting go mean just what the phrases imply. We urge you to initiate a new action plan for your relationship—based on doing whatever it takes to put the past behind you and reclaiming control over your lives for today and the future.

Don't be afraid to talk about old baggage when it comes up. Not discussing your triggers gives them more power over you than they deserve. Talking about the old garbage strips it of power and banishes it from your life.

In the next chapter we'll take this process one hard step further,

asking you to forget as well as to forgive. Now study the Passion
Points for more ideas to help you dump the past.

Passion Points

1. **Creative Dumping Power Workout.** Write on scraps of paper
    brief descriptions of old baggage you have recognized and have
    trouble shedding. Draw pictures, use photos, cut pictures out of
    magazines, or use any other method you can think of to make
    the descriptions as real as possible. Imagine all the anger,
    resentment, and other emotions associated with each bag satu-
    rating each description. Then burn the papers one at a time in
    the fireplace, or rip them into tiny pieces and throw them away
    in the kitchen trash. It is very effective to then clean your refrig-
    erator and dump all the "science projects" on top of the shred-
    ded papers.

2. **Work Out to the Oldies.** Train yourself to recognize when you
    are reacting to an "old tape" (situation or relationship) rather
    than a current situation. Some clues include:
    *   Feeling out of control of an emotion or emotions.
    *   Reacting totally out of proportion to a perceived wrong.
    *   Listing (mentally or verbally) all previous similar situa-
        tions involving your present partner and any previous part-
        ners, relatives, co-workers, or acquaintances.
    *   Saying or thinking universal statements ("every man,"
        "every woman," "everybody," "every time," etc.).
    *   Add your personal clues to the list. Once you recognize
        your reactions to triggers, do something different from
        what you usually do. For example, if you usually clench
        your teeth and turn red, go into the bedroom and pound on
        a pillow instead.

3. **Exorcise and Be Fit.** Alone or with your partner, gather can-

dles and incense. Beginning in the room in which you have the most emotional confrontations, light one or two candles and some incense. Mentally envision the subject of your last conflict as a ghost or spirit. Holding the candle high, command the vision to leave your home and your presence forever. Repeat in each room of the house.

You can make up chants to repeat as you do this. Some friends used this one:

Even though his name is Harry, I find his habits to be quite scary. Begone, begone ghost of my past, or else my new love will not last!

This exercise is not some esoteric occult ritual. Rather, it is intended to be fun, maybe a little silly. The important focus is to train your minds to visualize the banishment of your old baggage. Besides, candles and incense can be very romantic.

4. **Mid-Workout Hands-Off Temperature Check.** Tell each other often that you love each other. If this is something you don't do regularly, set goals. For example, one of you call the other at least once each day simply to say, "I love you. I was thinking of you, and just wanted to say hi." Don't discuss who's cooking dinner, how many stitches your oldest child needs this time, or chores.

   Advanced version: Promise you will respond with sincerity in the affirmative when your partner asks if you love him or her— WHEN YOU'RE ANGRY OR IRRITATED. This is highly intense training in separating your love from your reaction to a behavior or action.

5. **Deep Diving Conditioning.** During the day, each day for at

least a month, write ten characteristics or behaviors you appreciate about your mate. Exchange lists at the end of the day before going to bed. (Jack told Cyn he didn't believe she could list ten things she liked about him. She wrote one hundred and one items in less than half an hour. He still has the list.)

6. **Target Practice: Hitting Above the Belt.** Study these "Rules of Fair Fighting." Trust us—you can count on being tested.

   • *Remember, the purpose of a fight is to REACH A SOLUTION, not to win. There are only four possibilities: winwin, win-lose, lose-win, lose-lose. Fight for win-win.*

   • *Describe your issue, using "I" statements. ("I feel angry when you _____.")*

   • *Suggest an alternative or make a request. ("Would you be willing to do _____ instead?) Don't make demands or deliver ultimatums.*

   • *Agree upon a solution. ("I won't do _____ on purpose, but please give me some time to change the habit.")*

   • *Fight about ONE ISSUE AT A TIME. Don't move to another issue until the first is resolved.*

   • *If you are involved in a fight, you are probably not being paid to analyze your partner. Don't. Don't tell your partner what she is thinking, why he is doing something, or how he should feel.*

   • *In most cases, you are not a mind reader and neither is your   partner. Ask questions. If asked, do your best to answer honestly.*

   • *Leave past issues out of the current fight. This is not the time to share everything that bothers you about your partner.*

   • *Take turns speaking; don't do all the talking. Present one point at a time, and allow your partner to respond before moving on.*

   • *Do not call each other, relative's, children's, friend's, or*

*pets names. The only name-calling allowed is by affection-
ate names that you use at other times when you are not
angry.*

- *Don't stop until you have reached a solution, or have
agreed to table the fight until a later time. If you resched-
ule, keep the appointment.*
- *Always fight from a position of love.*

3 Forgiving and Forgetting: Can It Be Done?

Y ou've continued your inventory of your relationship and more fully understand some of the dynamics of letting go. Now you're ready for the really hard part!

"May God forgive you," said Elizabeth I to the Duchess of Cornwall, adding, "For I surely never will!" How often have you felt like that? How many times in your current or past relationships have you said similar words?

We are well aware of how easy it is to say the words of forgiveness. Often it becomes a way of life between two people, particularly those who are trying very hard not to let any real crisis develop that might tear them apart.

When forgiveness is so easily given, there may be something else going on. Forgiveness can be a weapon, and it can be a manipulative technique. If a husband forgives a wife for having an affair, then mopes around, closes her out of his confidence, and behaves as if he is suffering great pain, he is using forgiveness as a weapon. The message is, "I forgave you, but I cannot recover and I will make you suffer." The wife may or may not suffer as she watches her husband, but the husband definitely will suffer if his focus is on suffering.

If this same man goes a step further, he may use his forgiveness as a manipulative technique. She wants to go out to a movie with a female friend. The affair is long over, and a movie with her friend is her honest intention. He sighs deeply. "Okay," he says mournfully. "I was—well, never mind." The conversation continues, with her staying home because she thinks he thinks she's using the movie as an excuse to see her lover. He doesn't really think that but communicates that impression without really saying it.

Setting Limits

When forgiving comes easily and often, someone may be doing a lot of naughty deeds with no intention of stopping. Of course, this only works if the forgiver, for some reason, doesn't set very many limits. A man who has a problem with flatulence doesn't need to be forgiven every time he belches. However, his wife may set a limit by saying she won't go anywhere public with him unless he sees a doctor to find out if there is a medical problem. She can forgive him for embarrassing her at dinner with her boss, but there is a limit to her tolerance. Of course, he has to make a choice. She must allow him the freedom to choose, and she must follow through with her plan.

So when you have transgressed and your partner jumps in with ready forgiveness, we suggest you take it a step further. Ask your partner, "What do I need to do to be forgiven?" It's like hitting the tennis ball gently but squarely over the net into the opponent's side of the court. Your partner must take the necessary swing to return the ball. This way, you indicate you are willing to consider your partner's answer and limits if any are set. You also have valuable information to use in developing an action plan for being forgiven.

Cyn heard a story several years ago about a married man with a tendency to seek female companionship other than that of his wife. He eventually was caught and asked what he needed to do to be forgiven. His wife told him she forgave him and would move on without dwelling on past incidents. However, if he did it again, he was to deposit $25,000 per incident in her personal account. This was a reasonable sum, since the couple was well-to-do. However, $25,000 still stung. He didn't stray again.

Forgetting

Forgiveness comes in degrees of difficulty, as does receiving forgiveness. The really hard part in the equation is forgetting. How many times have you said to the love of your life, "Oh, sure, I can forgive what you did, but I'll be damned if I'm going to forget it."

The logical question then is, "If you're not willing to forget the issue, what makes it possible to forgive?"

Good point, we think. The churchman John Wesley once remarked that granting forgiveness but not forgetting the incident wasn't worth much. We have many examples of the times that all great religious leaders (Christ, Ghandi, the Buddha, the Dali Lama, Mohammed, Moses, countless popes) who have all exhorted the power of forgiveness inherent in mankind.

Compared to forgetting, then, forgiving is easy to do. Let's do a brief analysis of this process of forgiving and being forgiven. On the left below are the usual statements in a forgiveness exchange. On the right are what the underlying communication and intention should be.

I'm sorry.	*I did something I know hurt or offended you. I feel badly about it, and I promise to do my very best not to do it again.*
I forgive you.	*I understand what "I'm sorry" means, and I trust you mean it sincerely. For both our sakes I'm willing to put the whole thing*

> *behind me. I hope you will do the same so*
> *we can move forward without this being an*
> *issue again.*

The best way to keep the promises implied in the words "I for-give you" is to forget the whole incident. Later in this chapter we will share Jack's forgiveness pledge, which can be helpful in under-standing what's implicit in forgiving.

So we have put the burden squarely on you in this chapter. Namely, what will it take for you to forget the grievous act that resulted in asking your forgiveness in the first place? As we ask in the title of this chapter, "Can it be done?"

Can You Forget?

Emphatically, we answer "yes!" It will take a lot of work and it may not be permanently successful at first. Forgetting the act that caused the pain in the relationship (affairs or one- night stands are the most obvious) is one of the most difficult challenges for any person or relationship.

One reason forgetting is difficult is that no one wants to give up the advantage gained. As a forgiver who doesn't forget, you keep a weapon to use when you recall the incident and become angry again. And what a weapon it is!

You're feeling pretty good about your relationship, then some-thing trips you up. Your mind starts playing an old tape and sud-denly you're really angry again. You might even restart the fight just to release pent-up steam caused by recalling the incident.

Sounds kind of crazy, doesn't it? But it does happen, all too often. You finally resolve a crisis and exchange forgiveness. You reach a "let's-not-talk-about-it-okay-we-won't" agreement, and you begin thinking everything is going to be okay.

Then out of the blue something happens. Some minor incident activates the old issue and there go all your good intentions.

"I thought you had forgotten that," complains the offended partner.

"I had forgotten it until you got that phone call from your secretary. That reminded me of the last time a secretary of yours called at home when she thought I wasn't here," replies the armed, trigger happy partner. Just like that, you're right back on the battlefield dredging up all the old stuff you thought you had forgotten when you granted forgiveness.

If you are to "turn the other cheek" if a person strikes you, are you supposed to forget the fact this person hauled off on you? Would you be the slightest bit wary of this person, wondering if the fist is ready to strike again? How could you forget? Tough question, yet it's one of the obvious roadblocks in the way of recharging your relationship. Letting bygones be bygones is probably something you have to learn. Practice, practice, and more practice will be the order of the day.

We have a friend who is working on her relationship with her father. She went on in great detail about how she and her dad were working things out and how things were better than ever between them. This lady told us that she had really forgiven her father for abandoning her and her younger sister when she was six years old. The man had simply disappeared. He finally filed for divorce from their mother much later. He reappeared in his daughters' lives after they became adults.

"We go to lunch every other week now," she said. "Often he'll call and we'll see a movie together, just the two of us. Of course," our friend said, "I forgave dad a long time ago. But I'll never forget what he did to us."

Does she strike you as someone who has a healthy attitude about reestablishing a relationship? Any time things don't go exactly the way she thinks they should go between her father and herself, she has well-protected memories to justify her hurt and anger. She is on the right track to reestablishing a relationship, but she needs to forget his actions in order to truly forgive.

Think for a moment how funny it is to be angry at someone for something that they are not doing at the moment you're angry.

Naturally, a serious offense will take you some time to process and release the hurt and anger. The secret is to process the emotions and get on with your life and your relationship.

Consider your dog, or a dog you know. He doesn't hold grudges. He may snap or snarl or pout exactly when you do something that provokes him, but unless he's got other problems, the temper is a mere flash. Having lived with several dogs, we've noticed there is not that much of a difference between human and dog behavior. Dog behavior is simply much less complicated.

Again, setting limits can be very valuable to help the forgetting process. As we mentioned earlier, the person who erred is smart to ask, "What do I need to do to be forgiven?" The aggrieved party can then set some limits.

The big question, then, is whether you are truly interested in recharging. How persistently will you have to avoid forgetting?

Winning the Game

What you must do is thoroughly evaluate what you gain by not forgiving and not forgetting. If you're really mired in muck over something you can't forgive, the idea that you are gaining something by remaining stuck may sound utterly ridiculous. What could possibly be good about the way you feel when you can't let go?

Right there is part of the fallacy for many people. Having a payoff is not necessarily "good." Nor are payoffs bad. A payoff simply "is," just like a chair "is." Your behavior to get or avoid the payoff is what bestows a "payoff with power." If you continue to cling to your memory of the wrongdoing, a possible payoff could be sympathy. "Poor you. You were so terribly wronged. How could someone do that to wonderful you?"

People have a huge investment in being right. This is another one of those crazy dynamics in which we get caught. We insist we have the right to be right, and just to prove it, we'll say, "Remember when you . . . see, I was right about you working late with what's his face." Sure, we forgave. We're just determined to make somebody pay. During this same time, we will tell our friends and anyone who will listen that we want to be happy, to have a wonderful relationship, but why should we get involved again when we get hurt every time. Our question is (and believe us, we have to ask it ourselves on occasion), why keep the memory living when it does hurt? Who suffers? Is it worth all that suffering to be right? Is it worth losing your partner, your relationship, your friends—when everyone just gets tired of your chronic unhappiness?

Isn't it easier to discuss the problem, set some limits, then forget the whole thing like you forget a used tissue in the bottom of your handbag or pocket? That old injury has just about as much value as that used tissue, perhaps less.

We don't think any relationship will grow, much less recharge, if you are heavily invested in hanging on to the past in any form. When you continue to hold grudges and continue to look at your present partner through a lens smudged with ancient muck, then you have a very heavy investment in not forgiving or forgetting.

Growth Through Forgiveness

Everyone is entitled to make mistakes in life. Maybe we humans just say we're entitled to make mistakes because that's what we all do in life and probably always will. That's one of the ways in which we grow as individuals and as couples. We benefit from making mistakes by correcting them and not repeating the behaviors. So if recharging your relationship interests you, begin noticing the ways you behaved or reacted in the past and start making changes.

The mere act of forgiveness is in itself a way of making a change. If the "old you" was bent on holding a grudge and keeping that loaded weapon cocked, then a "new you" wants to say, "Hey . . . I forgive you, and I'll try everything to let this incident be forgotten."

So the act of forgiveness can be considered an act of change, and change is what recharging a relationship is all about. If you

continue to do everything the same way you've always done everything, what would cause you to think anything would be any different from the way it's always been—like a relationship?

Think about this: in the Roman Catholic faith, the words
uttered by the parishioner in the secret room of the confessional are
"Bless me, father, for I have sinned." The Church empowers the
priest, through the ancient heritage of the words of Christ, to give
or withhold forgiveness.

Does the priest really withhold forgiveness from the contrite
person admitting to being less than perfect? We hardly think so.
There certainly have been abuses of the power of granting and with-
holding forgiveness through the ages. To be sure, the Reformation,
started by Martin Luther in the Sixteenth Century, had strong roots
in the priests' abuse of the power of forgiveness. Those priests were
prone to sell their forgiveness as plenary indulgences. Pay so much
and you would earn so much good time in the eternal afterlife.

However, through the ages, humans mostly have sought to
leave ultimate forgiveness in the hands of a greater power. One can
still find court procedures in which the condemning judge will
close his or her pronouncement of a death sentence with the words,
". . . and may God have mercy on your soul."

As mere mortals, we may say that ultimate forgiveness rests in
the hands of the Almighty. If we do not believe in a Universal
Power, a God of our own human understanding, then we may say
the power to forgive rests with the aggrieved person.

Forgiving and forgetting can change the recipient as well.
Think of the times when you were caught "with your hand in the
cookie jar," for example. No matter what "cookie jar" you robbed,
wasn't there some time you begged forgiveness from the other
party? Especially when that person threatened to withdraw his or
her love, support, or companionship? Didn't the power of the relationship suddenly manifest itself and the importance of the other
person in your life become more clear? Did you think that you had
finally committed the act that could jeopardize or even end the rela-

tionship?

The old expression, "you never miss the water 'til the well runs dry" may have made the most sense to you when you thought your relationship would end because of something you did. Wouldn't you have done just about anything to be forgiven and even more to have the incident forgotten?

You really make a lifetime investment in anger when you won't or can't forgive. When you say, "I'll forgive, but never forget," you're really wanting to cash in on your anger investment. No relationship can recharge in that kind of environment.

As we've said before, you have to really work at coupling forgiving and forgetting, like linking boxcars on a freight train. Use whatever means necessary, but be certain you take the first step in the chain. That is, you must be willing to forgive.

Think of not forgiving as if you were determined never to let your partner "off the cross." Imagine that you have hung the offender on this cross for whatever sin she or he committed against you or the relationship. Just about the time the culprit works back into your good graces, you hang him right back up there.

A New Relationship

Forgetting a past grievance simply means it occupies no place of interest in your mind, in your life, or in your new recharged relationship. Fill yourself with the idea that the excitement of building a new relationship, one that neither of you has experienced before, far outweighs the short-term satisfaction you might feel by not forgiving and forgetting.

Let's consider our dog again. No matter what you may do to your dog—forget to put down fresh water, or food, or walk him as often as he needs—he continues to show you the unconditional love that sometimes you think you don't deserve. He or she forgives your unintentional oversights and neglects or long hours waiting for your footsteps on the front porch. Forgiveness is inbred in the animal. With a dog, you start with a clean slate every time, and doesn't that feel good? Do you think it's possible that you can behave on a level up to par with your faithful dog? Think about it.

In Jack's book, *Sex And Sobriety* (Simon & Schuster 1993), he wrote a forgiveness pledge. This pledge is for couples to use as they work hard to build new bridges back to each other from a fragmented or broken relationship.

The Forgiveness Pledge

I love you so much that not only do I forgive, but together let's let the incident be forgotten. I promise that I will not use it as a weapon against you. I will work my hardest to erase the incident from my memory, but if I slip, I will apologize to you and ask your forgiveness for bringing the pain back to your heart. I ask you to help me forget by not teasing or tormenting me, even in anger, with any remembrances that might cause me to bring the incident back to my mind. I pledge my efforts on our behalf, forgetting the past, forgiving the present, and exalting our future together.

(From *Sex and Sobriety*, Simon & Schuster, Inc, New York)

All Rights Reserved. Reprinted by permission.)

This pledge puts the responsibility on the couple to let the healing power of forgiveness work for them. Notice that it almost prohibits the little sniping techniques (teasing or tormenting) that many couples use like missiles. This sniping is dangerous because often one person's fun and humor is another's pain and anger.

Dr. James Emerson, a retired Episcopal minister, wrote in his book *The Dynamics of Forgiveness*, ". . . forgiveness can be defined as that dynamic wherein one becomes free to be a new creature." Think of the impact of that definition when you think about recharging your relationship.

Putting the fun back in, as our subtitle reads, does not just refer to a Disneyland of activities between couples. Rather, we'd like you to think of new ways of making changes as also being fun. When your thinking is clouded with old tapes and an inability to forgive, it's pretty hard to see any fun at all in a relationship. You've simply invested too heavily in the anger of the past to even think about having fun with your partner.

Thus, seeing how you can take positive steps to forgive and forget opens the door for fun to enter your life again. You find that by forgiving you are becoming a new creature. By forgiving and forgetting you invite all sorts of possibilities to feel more secure by letting go of old hurts. You begin to feel as if you can, after all, be passionately positive about your new relationship. You can feel that it's really possible to hook up the emotional battery cables that will help you begin the recharging process.

Passion Points

1. **Finger Flex.** In your own handwriting, copy "The Forgiveness Pledge" from this chapter. Put it someplace where you'll see it first thing in the morning and last thing at night. A good place is on your bathroom or vanity mirror. The important thing is to copy by hand yourself. Read it frequently.

2. **"Forget To" Exercise.** Think about a few recent times when you've forgotten something, like your keys or an appointment. (If you've forgotten what you've forgotten recently, you can probably skip this exercise.) What was happening when you forgot? Did you have too much on your mind? Were you just thinking about something else? Whatever happens to cause you to forget without trying may be able to consciously help you forget on purpose.

   Write down a few statements you can keep with you all the time and post in several different places—your bathroom mirror, the rearview mirror in your car, on your desk, or on you computer screen. Read these statements whenever you catch yourself thinking about what you want to forget. Use anything that makes you feel good or that you like to think about. Some

suggestions are:
- I have the power to change my thoughts.
- Right now I am thinking about what I'll plant in my garden (build in my workshop, fix for dinner, do for my birthday, etc.).
- I am a strong and powerful person, and I choose what thoughts control my life.
- When I think of (the incident), the thought will flicker through my mind and disappear like lightening.

Any affirmation about an area of your life you want to improve is appropriate. Simply concentrate on it instead of on what you want to forget.

3. **Healthful Heaving.** This exercise is for times you're really having trouble forgiving and/or forgetting. Plan at least thirty minutes when you can be alone and take a long, hot bath. Put lots of bubble bath into the water. Lay back in the tub, close your eyes, and take a deep breath. Start speaking aloud all the anger, hurt, frustration, sorrow, fear—anything you feel when you think about what you want to forgive and forget. Cry, shout, curse, whatever it takes. As you speak, imagine the words coming out of your mouth and falling onto the bubbles, causing them to snap and pop as they slowly disintegrate. Imagine the individual letters of the words dissolving into the bath water with the suds. When all the bubbles disappear (or you begin to feel as if you're sitting in a vat of acid), open the drain and watch the water swirl away. Imagine all the anger and emotion and words swirling out with the water. Say to yourself, "There. That's all gone for now. I feel better."

Repeat exercise as necessary. If it's necessary often, invest in some good moisturizing skin lotion or oil to apply after your bath. Imagine you are applying salve to your wound that soothes it and speeds the healing.

4. **Lemon Squeezes.** List a minimum of ten ways you can bene-
    fit from the incident you want to forgive. For example, you can
    be a stronger person, or you can stop being a victim. If you
    have trouble, look for articles or stories about people who tri-
    umphed over similar troubles.

For example, we have a friend (we'll call Lynne) who became
involved in a relationship not too long after the end of a relationship in which her partner cheated on her. They were living
together at the time, and Lynne had lived with other men with
either abusive or cheating outcomes. Her new partner wanted
her to move in with him after a few months of dating. She was
resistant to the idea, but eventually conceded and moved in
with him. Shortly after her move, Jerry began to feel guilty
about the way he had left his last relationship. He wouldn't discuss the matter with Lynne, but the implication was that he was
considering returning to that relationship. He didn't do anything other than meet with his previous lover on two occasions
(without sexual contact), but he was clearly struggling with his
guilt. Lynne was understandably trapped in some "old tape"
tracks. But she determined to do something differently this
time. She recognized that chances were about equal that the
relationship would either continue or it would end. Her list of
ten ways to learn from or deal with the situation included the
following:

1. Lynne took a personal inventory of her own self-worth.
    Didn't she deserve a relationship that included commit-
    ment and fidelity? She decided she did deserve that kind of
    relationship.
2. Lynne listed ways she contributed to the current relation-
    ship.
3. Without talking to her lover, Lynne made a list of what she

thought was making him feel guilty.

4. Lynne compared the three lists and concluded the situation was not about her or anything she did. This conclusion immediately helped her keep a high level of self-esteem.

5. Lynne made a new vow to trust the process. This meant that no matter what the outcome, she trusted there was a lesson for her in it and she felt strong enough to learn the lesson.

6. Lynne determined to behave differently under these circumstances from ways she had behaved before in similar situations.

7. She treated herself to long baths, a favorite relaxation for her. She cried, she raged at God and Jerry and anyone or anything else she felt anger toward during these baths. She sat in the tub as the water drained, and as it did she visualized all her anger draining with it. Sometimes she did this two or three times a day.

8. Lynne actually listened to something her mother told her, which was that she should concentrate on what she needed to do for herself and let Jerry do what he needed to do. In following this advice, Lynne allowed Jerry the leeway to make his own decision.

9. As Lynne did all the activities listed, she recognized her strength. As a result of that recognition, she realized she did not have to press Jerry for a commitment. She knew she would survive—and survive well—with or without him.

10. Finally, realizing that knowing something was better than living in a state of ignorance, Lynne confronted Jerry about his intentions. The critical part of this confrontation was that Lynne was absolutely clear that it didn't matter to her whether Jerry wanted a relationship and a commitment with her or not. She simply wanted to know the truth because she had been making plans to improve her life. She only wanted to know if he would or would not be part of those plans.

Talk to people you personally know who turned such a situation to their advantage and benefit. We know this is a little dramatic, but read a story about someone who is happy to be alive after a shark, bear, or crocodile eats a limb. Relationship damage may seem a bit less important. By the way, we loved the story about the woman who lost an arm to a crocodile, then when recovered ate crocodile at a restaurant. She said something to the effect of, "I'm eating an arm's worth of crocodile meat." This may seem irrelevant to our point here, but the message is that you can avenge yourself or get revenge without damaging the person you love. Be creative.

After you list your ten ways to benefit (known as taking that lemon and making lemonade), start making them happen.

5. **Spring Training Power Blocks.** Every time you feel the urge to bring up an old hurt, ask yourself the following questions. Journaling your responses and reactions to these questions is excellent if you're a journaler or want to become one.
    *   What's keeping me from forgiving? What's my investment in withholding forgiveness?
    *   Is my not forgiving going to advance our relationship or slow it down?
    *   Do I really need to withhold forgiveness so I can keep the loaded weapon cocked and ready to fire?
    *   What am I so afraid of that I feel I need to have and use such a weapon?
    *   How would I feel if he or she would not be able to forgive me?

4 Back-to-Basics Dating

When was the last time you had a date with your lover? When was the lasst time you prepared yourself as if you were meeting a lover? Do you limit special dates with your mate to the obligatory anniversary and birthday dinners? Do you think of your mate as your lover in all the romantic meanings of the word?

We first conceived of this chapter as one about dating. However, as we worked on it we realized we really wanted to bring out the flavor of romance and that special electricity between lovers that is available to those of us who have been together awhile. We will discuss dating, but we will do so from a context around you and your mate as lovers first, with spouse, parent, and other roles second.

Does the idea of taking your partner out on a date sound nuts to you? It is appalling how long it has been since most partners in a committed relationship, whether married or not, have put forth the effort to date each other. When we were researching and writing

Age Different Relationships, we discovered that most of our age different couples did actively date. It was one of the activities that made their lives exciting and rewarding.

However, when Jack is working with a couple in relationship therapy or leading a workshop about relationships, he always asks about the couple's dating pattern. The answers are pretty discouraging. We know how important this effort is in recharging your relationship, so fasten your seatbelts because we are going to fill your minds with some food for thought.

How Do People Date Today?

If you haven't kept up with dating protocol or etiquette, some current figures may be of interest. A recent survey conducted by Harlequin, the world famous romance novel publisher, revealed some figures that might surprise you.

Worldwide, women surveyed in most countries would be willing to initiate a date. However, American men responding to the survey opted for old-fashioned dating principles, at least when it comes to making the first move. Almost half the men surveyed did not want the woman to initiate the first date.

To Date or Not to Date

This survey information is important to set you thinking about what you are doing right now—today, tonight—to reenter the dating scene with your current partner. Think of how much fun you had in the early stages of your relationship. What made it fun? Maybe there never was much hassle about where to go skiing or bike riding. Maybe it didn't matter what movie was playing, or where. The important thing was that you were going somewhere or doing something. And you were doing it together.

What's happened? Well, you name it and it's probably happened:

"I couldn't get a babysitter.

"I forgot to pick up tickets, and they're sold out."

"I'm too tired to eat out."

"The movie got terrible reviews."

"Let's just watch TV."

"It'll be too crowded."

We'll bet you can list six different reasons not even related to the ones we listed. That's how certain we are that too many couples have not put much effort into recharging their relationships by dating.

Jack requires couples he sees in his practice to have one date a week while in therapy. They kick and scream and bring up all sorts of reasons they can't do this, but eventually he gets them to trust the process. That's what we ask you to do now. Trust the process of returning to the basics of dating. Here are some thoughts you can play around with.

If you made a list of all the activities available in your city that you've always wanted to do but haven't, what would the list contain? Art museums, concerts, or exhibits might be on your list. Don't think that you have to be in a large city for this list to have substance, either.

How many of you living in rural communities have passed up town celebrations each year because you didn't feel like going? Don't leave anything out of your thinking at this stage, but let your mind run free. If it's something you've wanted to do or it's something that has appealed to your idea of a good time, then run it around in your mind. See how it feels to imagine you and your partner actually going to that event, concert, or celebration.

Preparation

Then (and this is an equally fun part), think of what kind of clothes you would like to wear to any of these functions. Imagine yourself shopping for something new to wear on a date for the particular event you select. Go shopping in your mind. Where would you find the particular item that might be nice for your date? What about some nice bubble bath or some silky lingerie? This process, by the way, applies to men as well as women. Men should think about whether a new tie, a new pair of jeans, or maybe a sport shirt would be a nice surprise for both you and your date. Some new aftershave or cologne is always a good idea, too.

You don't have to spend a ton of money. A new piece of inexpensive costume jewelry, a new lipstick, or inexpensive earrings might be in order. Even treating yourself to a professional shoe shine or a colorful new pair of shoe laces for your running shoes might be enough to make you feel just a little bit special. You want to make your date feel special, to, by taking extra time on yourself.

Self-Esteem

These are little tricks to get you back into something you may have left behind for the last few weeks, months, or years. It's called self-esteem. Putting a little effort into planning a date helps not only to recharge your relationship, but also to fill up the waning reservoirs of your self-esteem as you prepare to spend time with your lover.

Now we know there are a ton of books out there about building self-esteem. Two, however, we find particularly compelling. We mention them so you can see what you may have been missing for a while. Also, this return to the basics of dating is a great way for you to begin focusing on your self-esteem again. We like Sam Keen's *Fire in the Belly: On Being a Man* and Gloria Steinham's *Revolution From Within: A Study in Self-Esteem.*

What makes dating a great vehicle for building self-esteem? You become the object of special attention, and you pay special attention to your date. You step out of the mundane daily routine and bring some pizzazz into your relationship.

Once a Week

We make it a point to have one date a week—a special and romantic evening or day. This means we stop whatever we're doing, take a few minutes to disengage from our work, and then start to get ready. Often this means we've decided to have dinner out on a Saturday night, braving the restaurant crowds like millions of others. So what's the big deal? Well, if it's a restaurant that we consider five star, we dress up for the occasion. Today's dress codes are practically unenforced, we've noticed. Some of the classiest, most expensive dining rooms say nothing when people wear their jeans or, God forbid, even jogging clothes to dinner.

We don't do that. Jack wears a sport coat and tie and Cyn wears high heels. We do it for us, because it's a special occasion just to be together treating ourselves to each other's company. We want to enhance the feeling of being special as much as possible. Especially because we, like everyone else, eventually have to return to the routine after the date is over.

Is it time consuming? Sure. Is it a bother to dress up? Of course, particularly when current trends are toward more casual dress. But the feeling that we are on a date is immensely rewarding, well worth the time and bother. We talk about things we have not talked about all week or even longer. We're positive, we talk about our dreams and plans, and we flirt with each other.

We each notice how the other person looks and we compliment one another about the way we have dressed for the occasion. We try to dress separately so whatever we wear on our date is somewhat of a surprise. We make an effort to re-create the moods we established when we began dating and were in the impressive and impressing stage of our relationship.

That's really what we mean when we ask you to recharge your relationship. By going back to the basics of dating, there is simply no way you can avoid putting effort into the activity. You step out of the stagnation in which your relationship has become mired.

Look at the advantages of starting to date your partner again. Sure, if you've grown a little distant you may feel awkward or self-conscious at first. However, you already know each other, so there is a comfort level there that you didn't have when you really first started dating. Yet you can re-create some of that excitement you felt back then. Be in a good mood. Look your best. Talk about fun topics and avoid your daily litany of troubles. This is not that kind of time. Woo, charm, and flirt with your date. If you're reading this book, you probably believe your relationship, your partner, and you are worth the risk and effort.

No Excuses

If you aren't dating regularly, what activities may be taking the place of an exciting evening with your partner. First on the list are really romantic activities, such as doing the laundry and cleaning the garage. Then there's work and the kids and the bills, and after all that you just want a little time for yourself. When you used to date in the old days, didn't you consider going out something you did for yourself? Didn't you have time then to plan and dress and be totally attentive to your date? Isn't your relationship even more worth that attention now that your have invested so much more in it? It's amazing to hear other couples tell us about their experiences of reviving their back-to-basic dating skills.

One couple went to a movie in a theater that happened to have a balcony. The cashier, looking at the couple, playfully asked them if they didn't want to sit in the balcony since "this is a very romantic movie." Believe it or not, the wife had never been in a movie theater balcony or experienced the reason for its romantic reputation.

Simply sitting in that balcony sparked a great evening for the couple. It made that simple movie date something really special. We know because they talked about it with us for weeks afterward. Added to the special memory was the discovery that they had been among the very last to enjoy that theater balcony. The entire structure was demolished soon after for a shopping mall expansion. This couple refers to that special, simple movie date as "our balcony date." The memory means a lot to them.

We have heard about some creative, inexpensive special dates as well. One friend invited her husband to meet her at a nearby hotel lounge one evening of a weekend when they both had to work (or so he thought). She actually stayed home, prepared a complete romantic dinner for two, and packed it in containers. A few weeks earlier she had reserved a hotel room during a weekend get-away promotion. She transported the meal, complete with candlesticks and tablecloth, to the hotel, and she brought with overnight essentials for both of them.

After bathing, applying makeup, donning a borrowed wig, and dressing in a sexy dress, she met her husband at the bar. As she sipped her drink, she slipped him the extra room key with a note suggesting he meet her upstairs. She left the table, and he joined her with surprise and appreciation for the meal, the effort, and the time together. He says he never thought he could get picked up by a sexy woman in a bar even if he wanted to, let alone not feel guilty about it. They still laugh when they wonder what other hotel guests thought.

Another friend with limited funds planned a special birthday date for his wife. He arranged for the kids to stay with their grandparents for the weekend, and he told his wife to be prepared to be away from everything for an entire day and night on her birthday. She was instructed to just trust him to be sure she had what she needed for the day. Furthermore, she was not to do anything even remotely related to work or home chores.

On the birthday morning, our friend "kidnapped" her. He turned on the answering machine, closed all the blinds, and isolated the two of them in their home. She was given breakfast in bed, a bagful of goodies, games, magazines, and little gifts. Two or three videos they both loved were rented for the day, and she was prepared her favorite dinner. He prepared everything, cleaned up, and generally waited on her hand and foot. Total cost was about $25. They still talk about the game of "Strip Hearts" they played with the cards in her goody bag.

Jack did something really special one year after Cyn had been delayed over a New Year holiday while visiting her family in Texas. Since we missed our traditional New Year's Eve dinner and dancing date, Jack covered two large pieces of plywood with inexpensive black and white tiles. He spread the tiles in the living room to make a dance floor. He made a special tape of romantic music for dancing. We dressed as if we were going out to a fancy party. Jack prepared a special dinner (complete with the obligatory black-eyed peas) and served it on a card table in front of the fireplace. It was one of the nicest ways to bring in a passionately positive new year either of us could remember.

Dating on a Budget

Remember that back-to-basics dating is not about spending money. Obviously you can blow a lot of dough and be very impressive about it. However, you can also pack a simple picnic lunch, hop on your bikes (rent them if necessary), and have a real blast just a few blocks from where you live. Try miniature golf without the kids. How about going to a drive-in movie by yourselves.

You may try driving to a neighboring town or a suburb to try a new place for breakfast on a Saturday morning. Would that be a date? You bet. And even more important, from the very first conception of the idea for the date, you begin automatically to put forth a little extra effort. Just knowing you're going out someplace, just the two of you, edging beyond your safe zones a little bit and risking someplace new adds a litle excitement. Before long, you'll want to keep that rediscovered excitement alive and growing in your relationship.

There are so many things to do as a couple that you have wanted to try but passed up for some reason. That's one of the things that makes this back-to-basics dating such a sure-fire method for recharging your relationship. How many times have you driven past the skating rink (ice or roller)? When did bowling become something you might want to try—either for the first time or again? There are concerts to enjoy and museums to visit. Do you really think the zoo is just for kids? We enjoyed the zoo so much that we had our wedding there with the giraffes in the background and the peacocks singing. It was different. It was unique. It was fun!

We have challenged couples we meet to find new and different ways to get back into the dating game. Sometimes bringing out an old board game is just the ticket. Couples can play gin rummy, cribbage, backgammon, chess, Chinese or plain checkers, to name a few. Incidentally, these are all good ideas for dates after the kids have been put to bed if you can't find a babysitter. So how does a date happen with a simple game?

Easy. You plan a wonderful picnic in your local park or your own back yard. Or try taking a board game to the library. They'll let you play. Just get out somewhere along with a board game and your lunch, your dinner, your snack, or whatever you choose. You've got a date. Don't know how to play? Great! Learn a new game together.

We try to play Scrabble regularly. The variations to that game are unlimited. When we are working on a new writing project, we play Scrabble by limiting the legal words to anything that has to do with writing or the subject of the book. We make a date by ordering pizza or going out for Chinese food before playing. Do we need to tell you the possibilities for using Scrabble as a love game?

Dating Differences

Here's one way to handle differences of opinion about what to do or where to go on a date. The first rule to remember is that this is a date. When you were first dating, you probably didn't raise too much of a fuss if your date suggested something that didn't particularly appeal to you. You went anyway because you were interested in spending time with this person. So, get back to that feeling of wanting to spend time together—special, private, loving time. Then what you do won't matter so much.

The real benefit is in the trade-off process of dating. Here are a couple of examples of good trade-offs. If your partner picks a place to eat that you don't particularly like, then you pick the movie you will see on your date. If the movie wasn't part of the deal, you suggest that next week the two of you will see a movie, and you'll make the selection.

Let's say she likes classical music and wants to attend a concert, opera, or a recital. You like jazz, blues, or rock. You go with her to the event she likes, and she goes with you on a later date to do something you like. In the spirit of dating, you'll have a fun evening because you can talk about each other's interests from a fresh viewpoint again. Sharing from a fresh viewpoint is something you probably have not done in a long time.

Exercise your perception again and consider this thought: When you focus on how little time you spend with your mate, or on all the reasons you can't or don't want to put effort into dating, those reasons become all you can see. There is no room for any other thoughts and no room for your relationship to have a chance to thrive.

Try refocusing your thoughts on your lover. Find time to be together because you want to be with each other more than anything. You may remember what a special gift you have in your relationship. Don't take it for granted. Take it on a date.

Passion Points

1. **You Deserve a Spa Break**. Have a spa date—you've worked hard so far. Take a bubble bath together, wash each other's hair, take turns giving each other a massage. If you don't know how, rent a video that shows you how and watch it together. Fix special, light, healthy snacks together to eat while you laugh at how you look in mud masks. Give each other a manicure.

2. **The Step (Out)**. Each weekend for one month, choose one of the following to do together:
    *   Have dinner and see a movie, play, or concert. Dress up.
    *   Rent a travel video of a place the two of you have dreamt of visiting. Prepare a meal appropriate to the place. Plan

what you will do and see when you go there as you watch the video.

- Individually, write a short romantic fantasy about the two of you and share the fantasies over a quiet dinner at home. Then act them out.
- Buy or make each other little gifts. Leave clues throughout the house that lead to the surprises.
- If possible, arrange to take an afternoon off from work. Meet for lunch, and do something you want to do but usually can't because of work.
- If the weather is nice, pack a picnic and go for a bike ride or a walk together. Spread your meal in the most secluded spot you can find. Don't forget sunscreen and bug spray.
- Do something totally off the wall. We went to the Federation Science Star Trek Exhibit in Boston and had more fun than most of the kids there. Go to an amusement park and ride the rides; do anything that allows you the opportunity to play.

3. **Advanced Perception Flex.** Remember the time you were most enamored of your partner. When was he or she the most charming, beautiful, handsome, or seductive? Remember everything you can about that time.

When you find yourself thinking more about what irritates you about your mate, drop the memory of your lover into place instead. Change the tape. Start by simply doing this self-reprogramming, and notice if, with a little time and practice, your attitude has begun to change.

5 Renewing the Spiritual

A person's spirituality is personal thing. It's an aspect of our persona that makes us feel somewhat special. Spirituality is the way we perceive the innermost part or soul of ourselves. Where do you stand with regard to the spirituality between you and your partner? If someone were to ask you to define your spirituality, what would you say? Would you say, "Well, we go to (church or synagogue) each week," or, "We used to go worship regularly, but we don't now." Would your answer even include religion or worship at all?

Spirituality is much more than church and religious nourishment. For couples, the ability to recharge a relationship is a holistic process, that is not just limited to the physical, mundane activities that make up daily living. After all, humans deal primarily with three areas in life on a daily basis: love, work, and play.

What is Spirituality?

When we talk of a couple's spirituality, we mean the part of their relationship that elevates them to awareness of the power of the God of their understanding, whether the Universe, Yahweh, Allah, the Great Spirit, the Higher Power, or whichever name closest describes their understanding. It is, we believe, more than being part of a congregation meeting for formalized worship, even though that piece of spirituality is also important. So when we ask you to examine your spirituality as a couple, we are asking you to look at the "binding of the book" of your life together. When the two of you watch a sunset, think about life after death, witness a powerful storm, wonder at a star-filled summer sky, or experience emotional events, what do you both feel? That's what we mean when we ask you about the spiritual part of your life.

We have found couples, particularly when both partners were previously in different relationships, often have fallen away from more formalized religion. Many times people with a new mate have drifted away from their family religion and adopted the religion of the new mate. Or they make only occasional and irregular visits to their home church.

However, couples who met each other through a formal church affiliation usually continue attending the church where they met. Of course, this isn't a hardbound rule. It just happens more frequently than not in these cases.

Interdenominational matches cause more problems. Will the couple go to his church or hers? Will they even go to church? Or, they might choose to visit temple or some other place of worship. Our point is that you can't dictate absolutely what must be done to build a spiritual life. Explore the possibilities. Don't rule anything out. There might be ways you haven't thought of to fill in some of the missing pieces that make up a truly recharged and holistic relationship.

There may not be a perfect solution, or the perfect solution could be very original. Back in the 1950s, a popular set of books titled *Gamesmanship, The Art of Always Being One Up* took a particularly relevant but irreverent shot at formal church attendance. When confronted with the fact that a gentleman always spent his

Sunday mornings on the golf course instead of in church, the gamesman was to reply to this effect: "As soon as man learns to build a cathedral that begins to match the magnificence of this great outdoors, then shall you find me among the first worshipers."

Finding Spirituality as a Couple

There are countless ways you can find the spirituality of your lives together when you investigate. Enjoyment and appreciation of the magnificence of the mountains, oceans, and forests are also forms of worship. Certainly a strong sense of spirituality prevails when you realize that a universal creative force pushed those mountains from the sea, carpeted the fields with lush foliage, and unleashed the crashing waves of the oceans.

If a couple walks hand in hand along a seashore, aware of the beauty of the ocean—the millions of forms of life that are within its watery walls and the mysteries of the sands of time that border it—then could anyone say they are not sharing a spiritual experience? We had such an experience in the early stages of writing this book. We had traveled to La Jolla for Jack to attend a workshop. Cyn put together picnic lunches that we shared on the shores of the beautiful Pacific Ocean. The breakers were enormous those warm afternoons, and we watched the sea lions and seals sunning, cavorting, and vying for a better sunbathing spot on Seal Rock a few yards off shore.

Gulls, which we don't often see in our part of the country, fought for our attention, catching bits of sandwich or apple in midair as we threw them. We held hands and laughed and kissed right in front of everyone. We were, in effect, having a spiritual experience. We both remarked how any troubles we were encountering in our daily struggles with the material world seemed so insignificant when we had the opportunity to enjoy the grandeur of nature.

We make it a point to travel to Santa Fe once a year, if possible. These trips are times of spiritual renewal for us. We visit the pueblos of the Santo Domingo or the Santa Clara. Once we climbed a steep trail to see the spectacular Nambe Falls, set deep in the heart of the Nambe Reservation. As we stood on the dirt ledge looking at the mighty falls, we could not help but wonder if we could hear the mighty voice of God in the crashing waters. Would anyone dare to tell us that we were not renewing our spiritual lives? Later, climbing down from the falls, we took off our shoes and walked barefoot in the icy waters of the stream below the falls.

We were lost in the beauty of this world, far from the cares of modern and hectic life. We felt very close to one another and to our Creator. We were thankful for the chance to experience this beautiful and simple lesson of what joy we can find in a committed and recharging relationship.

We experienced the simple, yet overwhelming, awareness of the presence of a greater power in a non-worship setting at the Santa Domingo Mission Church. We have sat with a well-known artist friend, a full-blooded Ciricaua Apache, and listened to him speak of his visions that inspired his wondrous scratchboard art, copies of which adorn the walls of our home. With his giant tepee silhouetted against majestic multicolored cliffs, he talked of visions and of living and dead spirits as we sat on the banks of the Rio Grande River at Embudo Station. We listened to the recorded Indian flute music of John Ranier, and it would be most difficult, to say the least, to convince us that we were not experiencing a rebirth of individual spirituality.

Finding your peace together, anew, is where spirituality leads a couple. Spirituality doesn't always appear in humanmade structures, but it often comes with recognition of the oneness born out of love, devotion, and even tears. The sure knowledge that there is strength in being a couple can happen anytime, anywhere, during one of these spontaneous spiritual experiences.

How long has it been since the two of you observed a sunset? A dawning day? When was the last time you held a baby? Played with a newborn puppy or furry kitten? When did the two of you last walk with a grandchild holding your hands? Have the two of you allowed a zoo animal to nuzzle against you or eat from your palm?

When did you both ease a fishing line into a mountain stream to test your wiles against a Rainbow or German Brown? Has life been so hectic that neither of you remembers the one hundred or more recipes for Spam prepared over a campfire? When was the last time you lay on the grass next to each other, gazing into a cloud-filled summer sky, swearing you could see the face of God?

Spirituality for the recharging relationship is what remains after all the Christmas presents have been torn from their nests beneath the tree. It is the invisible chain that binds your hands together as you listen to a homily or a full-blown sermon, or hear the clear, concise, lyrical voice of a cantor.

If a formal worship setting is what you both like, have you thought of looking for a new place to share formal worship? We are not advocating that everyone leave their home church or synagogue to find a new place. We are suggesting that you might be surprised at the boost to your relationship by finding a new worship place together. If you haven't attended services anywhere for a long time, ask yourselves the reason. Maybe a visit to another place or attending worship of another faith would be a spark relighting the spiritual ties you both may have neglected.

How many times have you heard your friends say they were raised Catholic (for example), "but we don't go to church anymore." Have you said that yourselves? Again, we are not equating formal worship with spirituality. Worship and spirituality are means to fill in the gaps in a truly holistic plan for recharging your relationship.

Think of times you and your partner sat in a concert hall, an outdoor amphitheater, or even a park with a bandshell, listening to music. Do you remember how your heart swelled with emotion at the beauty of what you were hearing? If it was a rock concert and you were swaying and clapping with the crowd, didn't you feel a sense of spirituality, albeit not a liturgical one?

Sharing the music-making or music-listening process—thought, emotion, love, struggle, life and death—can only help take you to a state of simply being. The spirituality of music can help when there are temptations to break your promises of fidelity. These temptations stand no chance against the knowledge that your relationship has such potential for greatness that you would do absolutely nothing to destroy it.

If you think about the spiritual meaning of holidays, there are many possibilities to incorporate your interpretation or expression of those meanings into a celebration of your relationship. For example, Easter or Passover can be a time to review tough times you've had as a couple and recognize how you've grown stronger as a result. Or, you can agree to overcome your challenges if they are still present. Use the holiday festivities as a catalyst to develop a plan to resurrect your relationship. You may consider counseling or simply spending more quality time alone together.

New Year's is an obvious holiday to make resolutions, which are statements that declare your intention to make changes. What about resolving to make your relationship passionate and fun again, or more so? Make your resolutions together, so you can support each other in your individual goals and make some to include both of you.

Christmas can be a time to celebrate rebirth. Consider the idea of having Christmas represent a rebirth of the joy of your relationship. The past is behind you. You can begin again, this time consciously, with awareness of the power you have to create your ideal relationship with your partner. Passion and excitement are great gifts to give your lover and everyone else you're around.

Cyn strongly believes birthdays and anniversaries also are holidays. They are the only days to celebrate you as an individual and as a couple. She celebrates birthdays not to measure years, but to be thankful that she's here and to consider what she's here to do. Birthdays can be wonderful times to adjust your perspective about the contributions you have made to those around you, even (and perhaps especially) in the less positive things you've said and done. And celebrating your partner's birthday is a superb way to communicate how special he or she is to you. Birthdays and anniversaries are also excellent alternatives to New Year's for setting goals and making resolutions to guide the direction of your relationship.

Spirituality and Purpose

Another aspect of spirituality is purpose in life. Some people have always known their reason for being. Some never do. We hear and read about people who know their life purpose. Tackling the meaning of your own life is enough to keep you busy, so we'll go ahead and add another question. What is the purpose you and your partner share as a couple? Why was your relationship born?

Of all the people in the world, the two of you came together. Your relationship is unique. If either of you were with another person, that relationship would be different from the one you share now. It takes both of you to generate the particular relationship you have. You have created something special. Why did you do that?

Like personal purposes for being, the purpose of your relationship may seem hidden, even nonexistent. It is a leap of faith and trust in some greater power, then, simply to choose a purpose. By doing so, you trust that you are guided to a proper choice suitable to the abilities, talents, and character traits pooled in your relationship. There are certainly enough people and causes that can use the power of your relationship.

If you haven't been doing much charity work together, choose something small at first. Go through your closets and donate old clothes to an organization that helps the homeless. Clean your pantry and donate canned goods to shelters at Thanksgiving, Christmas, or Hannuka. You can volunteer for a committee to clean up your neighborhood or raise funds for programs to help youth, eradicate cancer, or fight AIDS. After doing something small, try to choose something that is a stretch for both of you, to keep challenge and growth alive in your relationship.

Do something charitable, but do it together. Something mystical will happen. Your relationship will become bigger than the two of you individually, in a most positive way. Use your talents and skills that you may not fully use in your jobs or at home. You will discover qualities you didn't know you had. You may surprise each other and gain new respect for each other. You will probably have less time to fret about the little irritations and problems that seemed insurmountable before. Almost certainly you'll have more to talk about and have an enthusiasm that affects everything you do. Most of all, the two of you will be making a difference.

Spirituality Is Binding

Spirituality causes you to want to be reborn into a relationship that delivers on the promises that you once made to each other. Spirituality is such an intangible concept, yet it is so binding. If a couple cannot find spirituality, they may never find the true excitement available in recharging their relationship.

People using drugs talk of a spiritual experience at the apex of their high. Can you see yourselves attaining a spiritual high from discovering life—from a fresh, new perspective—without depending on drugs? Would you consider it spiritual to reach out to the needy, the homeless, the AIDS-afflicted? Would you consider helping an elderly couple in your apartment building or down the street spiritual? Would performing any of the myriad acts of kindness as a couple be something that would recharge your relationship and fill your personal wells of spirituality?

If spirituality can reaffirm the beauty of your life together, that's what we are after. The sense of serenity, the power of togetherness, and the strength of commitment could all be labeled as important elements of spirituality. In the dictionary sense of the word, spirituality is "of the spirit, of the soul." The goal is to develop and strengthen a connection on the level of your souls, in addition to your physical and material connections. Intimacy lives at this level, and sharing spirituality is a path toward this crucial aspect of a joyful relationship.

For you to fully recharge your relationship, we believe that spirituality needs to be present in whatever form you can discover together, formally or informally. Nurture and grow a unified dedication to finding spiritual peace together.

Passion Points

1. **High Reaches.** Do this exercise separately first. Charles R. Hobbs, developer of the Day-Timer System and author of Time Power, suggests the first step in goal setting is to clarify your unifying principles. Your assignment is to list at least five principles by which you live or aspire to live your life. What are your highest priorities in life? What do you value most? These are the goals you will never totally fulfill, but that form the network that supports everything you are and do. Some examples include:
   - Perfect myself spiritually.
   - Be loving.
   - Be ethical.
   - Strive for excellence.
   - Develop my mind.
   - Be open to new possibilities.
   - Have my presence make a difference.

   This can be a difficult list to make because you may not be accustomed to stating this type of goals. Obviously no one can always do or be all of the above examples. Also, we are trained to set a time frame for achieving goals. This does not work for unifying principles. Not even writing "by death" can accurately define ultimate achievement of these goals (although you may not pay much attention to them at that time). These principles form an umbrella under which all other goals nest and help define how you will approach your other goals. Aim for broad statements, but make notes about each if it helps.

After making your personal lists, set aside some time to talk about the lists with each other. You may want to adopt some principles your partner came up with. Then combine your two lists into a separate set of principles that define your aspirations as a couple.

2. **Stretch with a Partner.** Now make another list, this time of your individual skills, abilities, and interests. You can also include those you would like to develop. This is a composite list for you as a couple, although you can break it down into "his" and "hers" categories.

    As you review this list, think of ways that together you can use these skills together or develop these interests in a way that makes a difference. For example, if one person loves to sew and the other likes to work with wood, you could make wooden dolls together and donate them to an organization holding a craft sale to raise funds. The most critical part of this exercise: DO IT.

3. **Deep Breathing.** Each time you are going someplace together, make it a habit to take five minutes to stop along the way and look around you. In Denver, Jack and Cyn have ample opportunities to do this with the mountains changing daily and the huge reservoir park nearby. In some places you may have to think about what to look at. However, even in Cyn's west Texas hometown (flat, dirty, and dry), there were chrysanthemum gardens in the fall, awesome storm clouds in the spring, treacherous but pristine ice formations in the winter, and "vibrations" of the song of the cicadas in the heat of the summer.

If you're pressed for time, stop on the way back home. The point of this exercise, however, is to practice shifting your priorities from the physical to the spiritual, and to do it together.

4. **Vocal Cord Conditioning.** Try saying a simple thank you over dinner or another meal together each day for at least a week. This doesn't have to be a prayer, but should be some acknowledgement of what you do have. Say it from the heart. There may be those days when you're simply grateful you remembered where you live, or that you have someplace to live. Just say that.

    Have a mini-debate (NOT a fight) on the validity of this topic: "What you're grateful for you get more of; what you take for granted disappears." Try substituting "what you think about" for "what you're grateful for." Do some different things come to mind?

5. **Basic Eye Exercise.** Once a week, try to have a meal together outside or in some natural setting like a botanical garden, the zoo, or arboretum. Spend a minimum of five minutes not speaking, but simply looking around. After your meal, clean up your own trash and the area around you with the idea of leaving the place cleaner than you found it. This is a very simple, easy way to make a difference by being there.

6 Commitment

You are living together. Every time the word marriage comes up, you can almost feel the rivulets of sweat begin to run down your face. Is that such a great way to recharge your relationship?

So face it. Maybe you're just really afraid of the "C" word—commitment. What we want you to look at in this chapter is the myriad of reasons that make commitment so difficult. We'll consider what you can do to jump over this important relationship hurdle. Fear of commitment is important, because it stands between you and a relationship that is goal oriented. Such a relationship has a future attached to it, not just playing house with one another.

We have talked to couples who tried to convince us that they were just as committed as if they were in a marriage. We learned, however, that there was still an element of belief that they could just walk away from the relationship if it didn't work out. Does this mean it isn't easy to walk away from a marriage these days? Of course it can be done, and is. However, one must consider that there is expense involved in a divorce. When a couple can't justify a marriage because "it might not work out," then what are they doing trying to have a meaningful and positive relationship?

What if that doesn't work out? What if it snows tomorrow? Does one cancel his job, plans, or life because his plan for a sunny day was altered by snow? Probably not. Yet we hear this "what if it doesn't work out" all the time—mostly from men.

Why the Fear?

Some of the reluctance seems born from a failed marriage or several failed relationships, making commitment a really frightening process that these men don't want to go through again. Unfortunately, there are enough women who let them get away with it. So relationships just drag on for weeks, months, even years with no apparent goal of commitment.

Money can always be an issue—for a wedding or from a possible divorce. What's the difference? You can pick almost any excuse and make it fit your situation. Is it honestly enough of a reason not to direct your relationship toward a more lasting goal? Sure, you can argue, "Who says marriage is an ultimate goal in a relationship?"

To use a phrase that others have used, "If you're good enough to live with you ought to be good enough to marry." There's still a sense of trust, goal-orientation, and fulfillment of a destiny in the idea of two people proclaiming a legal commitment to one another. Is this a big deal? Sure, we think it is. It gives a couple the sense of direction that living together does not really offer.

Jack has seen couples in his practice who have been living together, even in co-owned houses, for several years. Yet when asked about the reason for not getting married (after eleven years of cohabitation), the woman replied, "What if it doesn't work out?"

There's almost no rationale for that kind of thinking. What would be the reason that two people would not make a serious commitment—that's recognized by family, friends, and the community as a marriage—after that much time? We can almost hear the resounding cries of those still living together saying, "But we have a committed relationship!" It's not the same. Why? Try this.

Think of the powerful weapon that is in the hands of either party when he or she can always say, "If it's not working out, then let's just break up." There is the not-so-veiled threat that either party can just pack and walk. Believe us, it becomes easier and easier to do just that.

We know couples who have been together for seventeen years, ten years, and five years. In each of these cases, one or the other partner has left the relationship not just once, but at least three times. Where is the stability in that? What is the missing ingredient? Commitment. It's just too easy to grab a suitcase and hit the dusty trail again. Then, when the other party gives in or there is a truce, the aggrieved party returns to the relationship. It's too easy.

What do you think would happen if leaving were not so convenient and easy? Isn't it possible that the couple would have to buckle down and work through the offending issues? We think so. One of the reasons we are so sold on commitment is that we know it helps recharge a relationship.

When a couple is in a committed relationship, they are eager to work on improving things between them. Jack always tells his people in relationship counseling that when a couple is putting more energy into deciding whether they should be a couple than into improving the quality of their lives as a couple, they are in trouble.

Joys of Commitment

We have been talking about commitment as it relates to marriage to get you cranked up about the meaning of commitment. In no way should you limit yourself to thinking that you have to be married to be happy or to be making a serious commitment.

Let's look at what may be going on when you bounce through one relationship after another and can't seem to hold on to any of them for very long. What makes commitment so difficult? Many men will offer excuses such as "I don't think I'm ready" or "I don't want to settle down yet." You've probably thought of these excuses and several others that you have either heard or used yourself.

Settling down simply means maintaining a monogamous relationship, providing nurturing, comfort, love, sex and companionship to only one person. People in today's society, frightened by the specter of HIV and AIDS, don't have very much casual sex or engage in hookups (one-night stands).

So why not settle down? Does an uncommitted person think she will be a lot happier if she can just move from one partner to another whenever the mood and temperament suit her? Probably. However, the excuse is always some variation of "I'm just not ready to settle down yet." As humorist Erma Bombeck has put it, "The grass is always greener on the other side of the septic tank."

If two people do not make a commitment to each other as a couple, then what chance does the relationship have to grow and become the nurturing and wonderful experience that it can be? We have asked couples what keeps them even from being fully committed to simply hold onto each other as the only partner for a while. Some of their answers are astounding as well as disturbing.

Probably the most inane answer we ever get as researchers is: "What if there is somebody better for me out there?" The plain and very simple answer is that there are probably thousands of people out there who are better for you than the person you are with. Do you really want to make the effort and spend the time, money, and all the resources available to you to go and find them? Rather than getting hung up on that line of thinking, why not put all that energy into recharging the relationship of the person you are with now?

This is a whole lot like the ritual of dealing with the *Sports Illustrated* annual swimsuit issue. If you are a smart man, we think you probably don't throw that issue at your female companion and suggest that you'd really like it if she could look like that. Better that you never make the comparison. Rather, make much ado about how you like the way she looks (swimsuit not withstanding).

Commitment also means having pride in being seen with and involving yourself with the special person with whom you are having a relationship. It says to the world, "Look, here's my very special companion, the person who brings happiness to my life."

Your goal in recharging your relationship is to reconfirm the commitment you both have to each other. Recently we saw a newspaper photo essay about couples who were renewing their vows at a promotional gathering staged by a local radio station. They were dressed in all sorts of outfits (including formal wear), going public again with their vows to each other.

Not all the vows exchanged were wedding vows, either. Couples not married but in committed relationships were exchanging words they used to keep enriching their relationships. How deep does commitment go, anyway? Sometimes it requires elaborate words, phrases, and eloquence to make commitment have enough meaning. Other times it is very simple.

We recall a marriage ceremony set outdoors between a young couple who had insisted on writing their own vows. When it came time for her to speak, she recited a very beautiful love poem she had written for her soon-to-be husband. After she was finished, the presiding judge turned to the bridegroom and asked him for his vows. What he said was simply, "We are!"

That was it. No addendum, no flowery sentences, but a simple proclamation of what he deemed a lifelong commitment. Would anyone argue that his two word statement did not carry as much commitment as her long and flowery love poem? Not on your life.

Being Passionately Positive

This entire book began when one of Jack's clients told him, "I would like to be passionately positive about my relationship." What a statement of affirmation for commitment. It carries with it the hope and joy and promise of what a relationship is meant to be. That sentence was the seed that began to sprout questions for us about what we use to recharge our relationship.

There is passion in the true sense of the word when two people make a commitment. It is the commitment that allows the no-holds-barred exchanges that express love, passion, and also disagreement. There can really be no fair fighting if there isn't enough of a commitment to want the relationship to be all it can.

The diamond industry has made its slogan, "diamonds are forever," as a means of communicating commitment. One gives a diamond as a symbol of commitment. More recently, any precious stone serves as a symbol of a lifelong attempt at a singular, focused, and goal-oriented relationship.

If there is no commitment, how can a couple create the future? How can a couple make any plans beyond next Saturday night? What excitement can there possibly be in planning a vacation when there is no guarantee that you will be together to take the trip? If you think this is exaggerated, think about situations when you were involved with someone who could not make a commitment.

How frustrating was it and how many times did you ask yourself, "What's wrong with me that I can't seem to get a commitment out of him/her?" Didn't you begin to wonder about your tendency to pick companions who simply couldn't make a commitment for one or more of a thousand reasons? And the reasons were always from the past, weren't they? It's not very flattering to think that you are going to have to pay for the mistakes of the past. It doesn't give you much of a jump start for your relationship, does it?

Think about training for the Olympics. Could anyone who seriously hopes to even be chosen to represent a country entertain such thoughts without commitment to the sport? We doubt it. In fact, most of the stories you hear and read speak of dogged determination and commitment to the sport, almost to the exclusion of everything else. This kind of commitment is not limited only to Olympic competitors. The movie, *Rudy*, told the story of a young man with average ability as a football player who was absolutely committed to playing football for Notre Dame. Despite discouragement at every turn, he did everything he could to convince the coach he should be on the team—even if only on the bench. At times he was criticized by the other players for working so hard during practices that his determination made the rest of them look bad. Yet during the last game of his college career, teammates and fans alike demanded Rudy be put in the game, and he was allowed in for one play. Rudy was the only Notre Dame player ever carried off the field on the shoulders of his teammates.

We often use the words determination and commitment as if they were the same. They are definitely dependent on one another. Being determined to win a sport, a promotion, or a contract means being committed to doing whatever it takes to achieve the goal. Thus, a committed relationship means that both parties are determined to do whatever is necessary to make their dreams together come true.

A committed couple is not torn apart by day-to-day problems or jealousies. They are excited about each other's goals in life. The committed couple is able to put their energies into recharging their relationship when they feel it losing energy. Further, they are able to do this without fear of losing the other person or losing their own identities.

Being in a committed relationship means feeling secure about who you are and about the identity of your partner. His or her ego is not going to take you down. You are not in competition with each other, but rather in harmony.

When we do some checking on the status of our own relationship, we sometimes talk about what makes us snipe at each other occasionally. It's usually a friendly skirmish, yet sometimes we say or do hurtful things that definitely do not promote the quality of our relationship.

However, we are committed to making our relationship everything that it can be. So we sit down and discuss this annoying little habit without the fear of destroying each other or each of our places in our relationship. Talking through problems in a committed relationship is considerably different from discussing them in a casual relationship.

Couples rarely put energy into what has no permanence. It just takes too much valuable time and effort when there is no definite objective to reach. Instead of wandering aimlessly through your relationship, consider the endless possibilities that await you when you overcome fear of the "C" word.

There is a wonderful sense of contentment, peace, and even serenity when you can say, "This is the person (relationship) for me." If you are stumbling over the "C" word, ask yourself, "What's the payoff for me that I cannot or will not make a commitment?" Do you always make sure you have some uncomplicated way out, rather than looking for a way to burrow deeper into a relationship?

It will be a definite boost to your ego and to your relationship when you can take a deep breath, cross over the line of indecision, and stand firmly at the side of your partner. Then you can realize that the two of you are committed to each other, with or without the benefit of formal wedding vows.

Your commitment is not only to one another, but also to the nurturing and growth of your relationship, making it a priority and treating it like the living entity that it is. Without commitment to each other and to the idea of being together, a relationship rarely can hold an initial charge, much less stand a recharging. Go on and cross the line. Get the "C" word over and done with!

Passion Points

1. **Mental Isometrics.** Make a list of your concerns about commitment. Remember that you have an issue about commitment if you are the one in relationships who cannot seem to make a commitment. You also have an issue about commitment if you always seem to have partners who cannot make commitments. Look beyond your current relationship as you do this exercise. You are looking for patterns.

As you write your concerns, write them as if they are totally your responsibility. For example, rather than writing "Women always want commitment too soon," write "I always feel pressured to make a commitment in relationships." Use your own words, but keep working at your responses until you can state them in "I" statements. Another example: "I seem to choose men who can't or won't commit" rather than "Men just can't commit."

Take some time with this exercise. Be really honest in your examination of your commitment issues. Only after you identify the issues can you take control of them and actually choose about committing rather than being controlled by your fears or biases.

2. **Acrommitment.** Write each letter of the word *commitment* on a line by itself. Create an acronym out of the word by choosing another word beginning with each of the letters that has some importance for you when you think about commitment. For example:

    C   Caring
    O
    M
    M
    I
    T
    M
    E
    N   Nurturing
    T

Leave enough space so you can jot down words for each letter as they come to you. Then select those that are the most significant for you for each letter, or prioritize them if you have more than one selection for each letter.

3. **Confidence Weight Lifting.** This is a good general exercise for
    building self-esteem, but it is particularly good if you have
    fears associated with commitment. For instance, if in Exercise
    One (Mental Isometrics) you listed phrases like "I'm afraid I'll
    end up with someone who is bad for me," consider how that
    fear is a statement about yourself that you are not capable of
    choosing partners who are good for you.

    You can strengthen your confidence in your ability to control
    fear—specific or general—by choosing something to do each
    day, or at least each week, that you are afraid to do. Jot down
    situations or actions that you face in your everyday life that
    cause you anxiety or perhaps you avoid because you are afraid
    for some reason. They don't have to be significant fears.

    Perhaps you'd like to try inline skating but you're afraid of
    looking like a complete spastic because you've never done it
    before. Or, if your first thought is of a fairly significant fear that
    you really would like to overcome, such as fear of public
    speaking, break it down into smaller chunks. Are you afraid of
    speaking in front of more than two people any time, or only of
    formal presentations? Are you okay with speaking in front of
    people you know but not in front of people you don't know—
    or vice versa?

    Now think of some things you can do to directly confront these
    fears. Perhaps you can take an inline skating lesson, or borrow
    a friend's skates and try them out in an office parking garage on
    a weekend when no one is around. You can get used to the idea
    that, yes, you will look like a complete spastic—and isn't it fun
    to laugh at yourself? Or enroll in a public speaking course. You
    might volunteer to demonstrate something you do well, such as
    a craft that can be used for fundraising, at your church or before
    another group.

As you make your list of fears and small steps you can take to chip away at their power over your life, imagine yourself being comfortable with discomfort. Begin to thrive on pushing yourself a little bit regularly to step outside your comfort zone. As you do so with some of these less paralyzing fears, you'll develop your confidence. Those really big fears, like fear of failure or fear of rejection, will begin to seem less intimidating. You'll be amazed at the freedom you'll begin to enjoy as you take the power of choice back from those debilitating fears.

7 Communication: What Does It Mean?

If you had to think of the one thing that seems to be bothering your relationship—this very minute—what would it be? Our guess is communication. Almost every couple Jack sees in his practice will identify that big umbrella word *communication* as the principal culprit in the failure of the relationship.

That doesn't mean that other things can't be wrong. It just means that communication ranks right up there with the major problems. We say umbrella because that's what this business of "we don't communicate" is all about. All the problems between two people trying to talk to one another, trying to listen to one another, and then trying to interpret what was said fall under this umbrella of communication.

For you to recharge your relationship with the added zest of improved communication, you must break up the word *communicate* and be specific about what you think is wrong. Just think of when the government broke up the Bell Telephone System into the "Baby Bells" and you've got some idea of how much easier it might be to handle the problem.

Does "we don't communicate" mean:

1. He talks but doesn't mean what he says?
2. She acts like she's listening but she's not?
3. He repeats back something you never said?
4. She interrupts you while you're talking?
5. He acts like he hears you, but doesn't?

We could fill up many pages of variations of what we'll call communications breakdowns. These breakdowns, plus the ones we didn't mention and the breakdowns that are very special to your relationship, are the reasons that we won't let you get away with just saying, "We don't communicate."

Define Communication

So, to recharge, get the old blue editing pencil out and define what you mean by *communicate.* Make a list of the behaviors that bother you the most when you try to talk. Prioritize this list with the most important behavior at the top and the least troublesome at the bottom.

When you have made your list, try to get your partner to make a list. Then the two of you compare to see if anything matches up. When you find a match (and you will), that's the item to start working on. Here's how you do it. You and your partner will start by making a new third list that combines the thoughts from each individual list.

Once again, these should be in order of importance. Once you have your combined list, make a copy so each of you is now working off the same list. Put it aside for the moment and let's address the question of what happens when one or the other of you simply won't talk at all.

This is simply not acceptable when a couple is trying to recharge their relationship. We assume that both of you are interested in doing this, or one of you wouldn't have bought this book. At any rate, here's a tool to use around the issue of your partner being noncommunicative. Ask: "Could you tell me what would make it possible for you to talk to me about (name the subject or the issue at hand)?" Please notice the difference between that statement and this one: "Why won't you ever talk to me?"

Don't Ask "Why?"

This last question is a clear invitation, through the use of the word why, to have your partner become defensive. Up goes the protective armor. So, please eliminate the word *why* from your personal communication vocabulary. When you use why, that's as far as any conversation will get. You are better off to follow our format and address the issue squarely.

By asking your partner to remove his or her own personal roadblocks to conversation ("what would make it possible . . ."), you are saying that you recognize something is preventing your partner from being able to share with you. You don't know what that something is, so you are simply asking him or her to tell you what you could do to help break up the log jam.

It might be something simple like, "I hate it when you try to talk to me while my favorite show is on." Or it could be more complicated. "You intimidate the hell out of me!" Either way, it's important for you to find the reason (not why) conversation is not happening. Then the challenge is to correct the problem.

Let's take that last hypothetical statement that your partner may have made, that you "intimidate the hell" out of him or her. How would you respond to that? For one thing, you certainly don't want your answer to be intimidating, do you? So, it will be important that you continue in the same questioning manner. For example, you might say, "It would be really helpful if you could tell me exactly what I say or do that makes you feel intimidated."

Now what you are setting up is a real exercise in effective communication. You are acknowledging, without becoming defensive, that what your partner says is valid. Instead, you have subtly recognized the behavior and moved right into trying to have your partner identify exactly what he or she sees and hears when you begin to talk.

You could dance around that maypole for a long time and never really reach the exact behaviors your partner sees. It's close enough that your partner feels intimidated when the two of you are trying to talk. What you are going to do is help resolve that feeling if possible. When you ask your partner to tell you what you are doing or saying that seems intimidating, you are getting into his or her agenda without defending your own actions. The point is not to justify what you do, but to discover what you do.

It isn't as complicated as it may sound at first reading. Let's look at another simple example of how you can reach your partner's agenda about difficult communications with you. Let's say that you offer to go get ice cream cones. You ask your partner, "How would like me to get us an ice cream cone?" Your partner responds with the hearty thrill of anyone about to get a present.

However, you fail to ask him what flavor he would like. Instead, you sound like a commercial for Baskin-Robbins as you begin to name all the flavors of ice cream you can think of besides the one your partner wants. You might actually almost get up to thirty-one and still not mention the flavor or combination of flavors that your partner wanted. Get it?

Unblocking Communications

As long as you persist in offering reasons for, excuses for, and ideas about whatever is troubling your communications, you probably never will discover what your partner is feeling. Hence, communications continue to be blocked.

Let's take another example of how you can unblock another communication snafu. In the rules of fair fighting that we gave you in Chapter Two's "Passion Points," one of the principle rules was "to seek a solution." This means that neither you nor your partner have to defend a position of right or wrong. What you are after is a solution to whatever problem you are discussing.

Therefore, in the discussion between the two of you, be very careful about using accusatory statements. Avoid questions that will put your partner in a position of having to be right and make you wrong. Usually this happens when one person starts getting into what we call universal language.

Universal language consists of phrases you use in communications such as, "You *never* (universal) do such and such . . ." or, "You *never* (universal) let me finish," or "This happens to me *all* (universal) the time."

Universal language has such unlimited power that your partner must immediately scramble through his or her mind to try to find just one occasion when he or she didn't do, say, or act the way you have suggested. *Always, never, all,* and other universal triggers start that mind scramble, so avoid them. Try being very event-specific by saying, for example, "Last night when I wanted to be cuddly, you said you were too tired." That's a direct, time-specific statement. Listen to the difference in a universal statement: "You are always too tired to even cuddle with me."

Here's another event specific example: "At your last birthday party, I was really upset because you seemed to be such a kill-joy after I had worked so hard to give you a happy day." That's pretty event- and time-specific. It also says exactly how you feel (upset) about the behavior of your partner. Compare that statement with this universal one: "I'm never going to give you another birthday party, because you're always such a kill-joy." A statement like that not only contains two universal language words (never and always), but also automatically accuses your partner of a behavior. It doesn't address your feelings about the event. What kind of communicating would you expect to come from something like that?

We can assure you that it would be a long fight that might never be resolved. Instead, you would volley back and forth about who was right and who was wrong. Continuing with that example, it could go better with this approach: "At your last birthday party, I sensed (softer and more acute than felt) that you weren't having much fun. I wondered what that was all about. Can you tell me or was it really just my imagination?"

Now there's an open invitation to some good, feeling-level conversation. We can imagine your partner replying by saying something like, "Well no, you were right (acknowledging your feeling). I wasn't having much fun. Guess it was because this is the last year I'll be in my thirties. I didn't realize that I was spoiling everyone else's fun." You can respond by asking if your partner wanted to have another party this year since last year was so dismal.

What you do when you learn this kind of communicating technique is you stop going for the ace tennis shot. Instead, you settle for lobbing the ball consistently and steadily back over the net of conversations with your partner.

Think of it this way. It really doesn't take much skill to slam the lofted ball down your partner's throat. That takes more brute strength than skill. Returning each shot hit to you is much more skillful and will eventually be easier and less tiring. It is the same with communicating. Just returning the ball, or addressing the question or the statement made by your partner, is a lot more effective than trying for the slam shot.

Improving Communication Skills

Communication, we're sure you'll agree, is a very large umbrella indeed. What you're looking for is improvement in your skill levels. For example, try creative listening—the ability to really understand what your partner says to you. Here's how you do it.

During a fair fight or regular communication, it can be difficult to make sure that you heard correctly what your partner said. Use this tool: "If I understand you correctly, you are saying . . ."

This underscores that you heard exactly what your partner said and that there are no misunderstandings. An example might be:

SHE: "I really have a difficult time with the way your mother talks to me on the phone."

HE: "You never have liked to talking to my mother."

Obviously, he isn't listening at all to what she just said, but he is hearing only part of the message, the bad part at that. If you use the creative listening tool, it would go like this:

SHE: "I really have a difficult time with the way your mother talks to me on the phone."

HE: "If I understand what you're saying, you wish Mom would talk to you on the phone differently. Is that right?"

You might think that sounds pretty awkward, but it really works. It forces you (HE in this case) to make sure you heard exactly what your partner (SHE) said. Rather than ending up in left field with a lot of defensive stuff about families and all the other garbage, HE wants to hear from SHE what bothers her when SHE talks to HIS mother.

If you think nobody says, "If I understand you . . ." remember you are trying to use new tools. When you actually start doing this, you'll find how easy it is to use words and phrases that help you and your partner communicate in a more effective and creative manner.

Use Timeouts

We use the timeout signal with one another when we find an argument appears to be turning into a full-blown unfair fight, or when we're getting off the subject. When you use the timeout signal, cross one hand over the extended fingers of the other hand in the shape of a "T," just like in sports events. The trick to using timeouts is the other person must agree to honor such a gesture. That's something both of you should agree will happen before you begin any serious attempt at improving communication and creative listening.

The timeout does not mean you drop the subject—only that you are seeking an interruption to what your partner is saying to clarify a misstated point or fact, or to keep the discussion from getting off track. We also use the timeout as a means of saying, "This discussion is making me angry and I'm losing perspective. I would like to stop this discussion temporarily, and we can talk about it later."

Follow the rule of the timeout, however. It is a temporary cessation of conversation—discussion or fair fighting—not a permanent end to the subject. Too many couples, we find, use the timeout as a means to just walk away from the argument or discussion, never to return to it.

Time and Place Are Important

One other effort is important in recharging your communications. Choose the place and time to talk carefully. Always try to be comfortable when you have serious discussions, conduct a fair fight, or try to resolve a communication block between you.

You always feel safer if you have difficult conversations happen in a public place such as a restaurant. You are less likely to shout or get carried away with rhetoric if you are in public. You'll tend to use creative listening tools, which help you arrive at more satisfactory conclusions to your communications. You have the opportunity to have your conversations be complete and resolved instead of fouled up, hanging in the air with no decisive answers to the problems presented.

If you are seriously communicating at home, then do it in a setting where there are no distractions—no kids (if possible) and absolutely no TV or radio. Turn on the answering machine or whatever you do when you don't answer the phone. And set a time limit for the discussion. We are both comfortable in our living room, usually with Cyn curled up by the fireplace and Jack sitting on the floor with her or in a chair opposite her.

The time of day you pick should not be very late at night or very early in the morning. Take into account your biological clocks when choosing a time to have a serious discussion. Lunch is good. Lunch out is even better if you can arrange it.

Finally, don't be afraid to use notes for a discussion. It's far better to stick to an agenda for your discussion and arrive at solutions than to just start flailing away at one another over every little hurt or slight that may get mixed in with the really important topics for discussion. Using notes is an especially effective tool if you have had trouble keeping your thoughts straight during potentially stressful discussions. With time, practice, and a caring partner you will eventually learn to stay on your mental track, even under pressure.

The Ten-Minute Drill and Fair Fighting

We call this technique the Ten-Minute Drill (originally described by Jack in his book, *The Joy of Being Sober*). One of us says, "I've got an issue. Can we talk about it?" In the Passion Points for this chapter, you will learn the Ten-Minute Drill technique for dealing with issues to arrive at answers. But for now, a written note about precise complaints or topics will help improve the quality of your communication while recharging your relationship.

There's absolutely nothing like a healthy, fair fight to recharge any relationship. It's healthy to learn how to really use these tools for improving communication and to more specifically pinpoint what has been keeping you and your partner from having a better relationship through talking, listening, and acting on suggestions for making things better between you.

Discussing issues, sometimes fighting, can make some people uncomfortable. Consider, however, that fighting doesn't mean you don't care about your partner, or vice versa. It means that you care enough about the relationship to fight for it. You care enough to do what it takes to resolve issues and work out disagreements. Your commitment is to improving yourselves personally and as a couple by continually improving your ability to communicate—to reach resolutions rather than score wins.

Passion Points

1. **The Ten-Minute Drill.** We strongly urge you to use the Ten-

Minute Drill for discussions other than those that have resulted
in arguments before. Otherwise, the suggestion that "we drill"
can become an automatic trigger for "Oh, great, I'm in trouble
again." This tool is too useful in all types of communications to
become a source of dread. We use it for brainstorming about
projects (so we don't shoot down each other's ideas), for
resolving problems in our businesses, for making plans for
almost anything, and for issues that carry an emotional charge
for one or both of us. The Ten-Minute Drill is useful for any
conversation that requires input from more than one person.

The drill itself is simple. However, we have several tips and
discussion ideas that make this a lengthy exercise. We feel the
drill is worth the space and effort required to master it.

The basic drill is:
1. Choose a comfortable place with minimal distractions.
2. Set a timer for ten minutes.
3. Take turns speaking until the timer buzzes or you reach a
    resolution.
4. Reset the timer if necessary for another ten minutes.
5. End with a hug.

Now for the additional tips and discussion.
•   Find a timer that makes some sort of noise, such as an egg
    timer or the timer on your stove.
•   Manage your discussion time so that there are no distrac-
    tions of any kind during the drill.
    —   Turn off the radio, TV, and stereo.
    —   Send the kids to their rooms or next door, or have the
        drill after they've gone to sleep.
    —   Put the pets in the back yard or outside the room. Turn
        on the answering machine or unplug the phone in the
        room you're using.

— Don't answer the doorbell.

- Set your timer for ten minutes.

- The person with the issue starts first, with "I" statements. *I feel frustrated when I think you don't have time anymore for fun.* The first person talks until he or she has said everything that comes to mind, or until some response is necessary before continuing.

- The partner who has just finished says "Go" to indicate it's the other person's turn. Always use the same signal. Particularly during emotional conversations, you can miss signals or forget to give them unless you clearly agree to use the same one consistently.

- You can speak only during your turn. When your partner is speaking, use creative listening. Discipline yourself to concentrate on what he or she is saying rather than formulating your response or defense. Learn to trust that when it's your turn, you'll know what you need to say. If you're preparing instead of listening, then you're focused on winning rather than resolving.

- Use the tool mentioned in the chapter, repeating what you think you heard your partner say. *I think you're saying that you feel I'm not spending enough time with you doing things that we enjoy. Is that right? Go.* At times, you may find your turn consists of only one or two words: *Yes. Go.* Remember that you're finding a resolution, not impressing your partner with your rhetoric.

- This next tip may sound like we're encouraging you to stifle feelings, but it really is something that facilitates the effectiveness of the drill. Manage your face and your body as if you're playing poker while your partner is speaking. Don't roll your eyes, grimace, throw your hands up in disgust, or otherwise convey judgements or reactions. This accomplishes at least two important objectives: You allow your partner to speak without being distracted by your non-

verbal messages, and it helps you distance yourself somewhat from the discussion so that you can be proactive
rather than reactive. The exception is that an occasional
nod, a slight smile, and eye contact are positive signals that
you are listening, hearing, and validating your partner.

• Validation is an extraordinarily important part of the Ten-
Minute Drill and of communication in general. Your partner simply has the feelings he or she is sharing, and there
is nothing at the moment he or she is speaking that you can
do about those feelings. Later, you may be able to do something differently to help, but at that moment those feelings
are reality for your partner. Let them be. Your job is to simply hear the feelings as your partner shares them.

Don't get trapped believing that your own interpretation of
the cause of your partner's feelings is reality. For example,
if your partner says, "I just go crazy when it sounds like
you're telling me what to do," it's not very effective to
respond with, "You just have a problem with authority,
period." First, you are not responsible for analyzing your
partner's problems. Second, such a statement pretty well
shuts down any further effective communication. What
kind of response can there be? You've essentially just said
you don't consider his or her feeling valid because it stems
from an old tape or behavior pattern. The conversation, if it
continues, becomes about whether or not your partner actually does have a problem with authority, about your patron-
izing tone or attitude, how you don't listen and how your
partner can't communicate, and so on ad nauseam. We're
sure you've had the experience.

Much more effective: "*I wonder if this is part of your resistance to authority that you've talked about before. Do you
think it is, or is it something I'm doing or saying that makes
you feel I tell you what to do?*"

Then your partner can respond by saying, "*I thought about that authority thing, and that's not it. It's more that sometimes the way you say things sounds like I have no choice about the matter.*"

You respond, "*Can you give me an example so I can understand what you mean?*"

Then your partner says, "*Well, yesterday you said I should call Brenda to see if we can bring anything to the party this weekend. I planned to call her, and in fact had called her, but it sounded like an order to me. And I didn't have a chance to tell you I had done it before you seemed to just assume I wouldn't.*"

You then say, "*I didn't mean it to sound like an order. I was thinking about my to-do list and I wondered if I needed to put a trip to the grocery store on it, and I just said that without really thinking about how it sounded. I'll try to be more aware of how I say things to you from now on. I get so used to just telling people what needs to be done at the office that I sometimes don't think about the fact that you're not an employee and our relationship doesn't include permission to give orders. I'll do better. Is there anything else around that?*"

Notice that you don't address the authority problem directly again. That's not the issue. The issue is something you've done or said that caused your partner to feel a certain way. A resistance to authority for whatever reason may or may not be a part of the problem for your partner, but that's up to him or her to address and resolve. And he or she may surprise you by asking you to help with it. "*You know,*

*maybe I am overly sensitive to anything that sounds like
authority. I still go crazy when you say things like that, but
I'll try to be more aware of my reaction, too. I don't want
either of us to have to watch every word all the time. But I
appreciate that you'll work on it, and I promise I will too."*

This kind of effective exchange really happens. We've seen
it time and again.

• Let's go back to the beginning of our sample exchange and
assume you just can't help it—you have an emotional reaction. In this case, be honest and say how you feel, using "I"
statements. So, from the top, your partner goes crazy when
it sounds like you're giving orders. During your turn you
say, *"I can't help it—I feel that's unfair. I was thinking
about what needed to be done and not about how I was
saying anything. Sometimes (not universal, notice) I feel,
especially lately, that you're really sensitive about a lot
(again, not universal) of things I say."*

Now is a good time to take a breath and think about what
you've said. You haven't said "go," so it's still your turn.
Now you have the opportunity to go back to the tools and
keep the conversation on track. Remember, the issue is not
how you feel, but about your partner's feelings. You can
have your own issue later. Use the timeout signal and take
several more deep breaths if necessary while you remember the tools.

Now you can come back with honesty and your creative
listening tools. *"But this is about your feelings, so let me
see if I heard what you said. You feel I give you orders
sometimes. Can you give me an example so I can under-*

stand what you mean?" From here you are back on track. Later, if it's still a question for you, you can ask, *"Is anything going on lately with you that you might be a little sensitive? Is anything bothering you that you'd like to tell me about, or am I just imagining this?"*

You've validated your partner's feelings, and you've actively demonstrated your commitment to making the drill work by getting back on track. You've opened the door to intimacy and a safe dialogue. Now your partner can feel free to share if there is something going on, whether he or she is being sensitive or not. It may be pressure at work, pressure with the kids, worries about money, even an old fear of abandonment or rejection. Or there may be nothing at all. The gift is that you have provided an opportunity, you've listened, and you've shown that you care.

2. **The Stick Workout.** This is something the two of you can do together that is creative and useful. Take a walk together and look for a fairly smooth or smoothable stick that feels comfortable to both of you. The go to the craft store and buy some neat decorations to make a Talking Stick. If you use the style of the Native American source of this idea, you'll need things like leather strips, feathers, some charms or other decorations, and some good craft glue. Just look for items you like, and both of you should select some of them individually as well as jointly.

Then make your stick, attaching your feathers and decorations with the rawhide or ribbon and glue. Do this together also. It doesn't matter what you use as long as you both create the stick together. However, if you're interested in some folklore and symbolism, here are a few things to consider incorporating. (Please note the following mostly lie in the domain of folklore and are not scientifically proven; at the very least using some

of these symbols makes an interesting and attractive Talking
Stick.)

- Mercury: mythological messenger of Jupiter.
- Astrology: Gemini is the sign of communications, Cancer
  of the home environment, and Libra of marriage. Mercury
  is the planet of communications and mental activity nad
  Venus is of attraction, love and creativity.
- Colors: White represents protection, peace, happiness, and
  spirituality. Brown represents the home. Pink represents
  emotional love, fidelity, friendships. Yellow represents
  mental powers and wisdom. Red represents courage,
  strength, and power.
- Gems, Stones, and Metals: Quartz is the stone of power,
  focus, and elevated thoughts. Rose quartz is specific to the
  heart and increases feelings of self-worth. Turquoise represents protection and fidelity, aids mental relaxation, and
  calms emotions. Cat's Eye and Tiger Eye stimulate clear
  thinking and discernment. Coral promotes a sense of well
  being. Green Jade stimulates practicality and wisdom.
  Obsidian, or the Apache Tear, provides protection for the
  sensitive. Sodalite dispels guilt. Copper prevents a negative
  attitude. Gold promotes self-acceptance and self-enhance-
  ment. Silver promotes self-improvement.

There are certainly more symbolic images you can use—religious symbols, for example, or favorite items you may have
received as gifts or that have special meaning for one or both of
you. You might also want to glue or paint reminders to yourselves on the stick, such as "Go," "I" for "I" statements, an ear
for creative listening, and so on.

You will use your Talking Stick during any conversation that is
important to either of you, when you find yourselves interrupt-
ing each other out of excitement or strong emotional responses, or anytime you just feel like it. The stick is not for hitting or

throwing at each other. Use it during Ten-Minute Drills as further reinforcement of your commitment to fully listening to each other. Whoever has the stick has the floor. We do suggest you observe the rules of fair fighting and the rules for the Ten-Minute Drill when using the talking stick for those purposes.

Finally, your Talking Stick is a work of love and art (no matter what it looks like). Keep it in a special place, preferably on display and where you can get to it if you suddenly find yourself in need of managing a conversation. We think this is also an excellent tool for family communications.

8 Care: Giving and Getting

It's absolutely amazing how codependent we can become in a relationship. Codependence is such a buzzword these days that it is applied to a multitude of circumstances—from the person living with a chemically dependent mate to the secretary covering up for a boss. One of our favorite definitions of codependence is, "I'm so codependent I'll take the grocery cart with the broken wheel so you don't have to."

Does the term codependent apply to a relationship when you do little things for one another that you think are caring, but someone else says are codependent? The term probably does apply sometimes. Codependency certainly has an impact on how two people perform in the little playlet that is their relationship.

Caring covers a wide spectrum of behaviors that mean different things to different people. If I lay out your raincoat and umbrella, am I showing care for you or am I taking care of you in a codependent way? If you remind me that the house mortgage is due today, are you caring for our relationship, or are you being codependent? Drawing the distinction can drive you nuts.

So let's just say that we'll leave all your possibly codependent behaviors to you and let you deal with whatever issues they may bring up. To really recharge your relationship, however, caring must be an integral part of daily living for both of you. Frankly, we don't care if some call caring behavior codependence. Now, what do we mean about the importance of caring?

What Is Caring?

Do you really want to be in a relationship if you feel that you can do whatever you want and nobody cares? It sounds great on the surface, but isn't it really discounting when no one ever asks where you've been, what you've be doing, or who you were with? When no one cares enough to ask those questions, don't you feel like maybe you're not making any impact on this relationship? Don't you wonder who gives a damn whether you're there or not?

Caring, as applied to recharging your relationship, is the myriad of acts performed by everyone who says, "You are really important to me and I want you to know it. I show this by doing little things that are concrete proof of my care."

Is the Boy Scout who helps the elderly person across the busy intersection showing care, or is he enabling the elderly person to avoid crossing streets by himself? The questions can get crazy and bogged down in psychobabble when you try to analyze every behavior you perform in your relationship. Making certain that everything you do is healthy can make you sick.

We think you should trust your instincts about caring. Put into practice the knowledge you have learned over many years. For example, whatever happened to your knowledge of The Golden Rule—do unto others as you would have them do unto you? How many times did you hear, "Treat other people like you want to be treated," or the more colloquial, "You rub my back, I'll rub yours."

From the time our life script is written around age four or five, we begin to assimilate all the attitudes, proverbs, curses, promises, and quotations that help form us as unique people. We enter a relationship loving one another and certainly lusting for one another, but are we caring for one another?

In our relationship, asking how the day went for Cyn and Jack is not something we say just to hear the sound of our own voices. We genuinely care what happened to each other. As a result of that caring, we usually talk on the phone, albeit briefly, several times during the day and evening. We both work such crazy hours, writing at different times, swapping pages and computer discs, that we need to take the time to care what the other is doing.

A big step for our own recharging came when we decided to try to have lunch together as often as possible during the week. This is our time to communicate on a feeling level and put some energy into our relationship. Nights are mostly failures for sharing because Jack doesn't get home from seeing clients until almost 8:30 p.m., hardly making him the ideal dinner companion.

Cyn stays up most of the night writing or working on some other project, and might be in bed by 3:00 or 3:30 a.m. Jack usually gets up at 4:00 a.m. so he can read and write. He would like to have many complicated conversations at any time in the morning up until about 3:00 p.m. Then he takes a twenty- to forty-minute "wolf nap" to get ready for the evening run of clients. Cyn doesn't want to even nod in agreement before 11:30 or noon, and would prefer not to begin any interaction until about 3:00 or 4:00 in the afternoon when her biological clock is gearing up for the evening.

This "owl and lark" relationship means that we have to genuinely care about whether things are going okay for each other. We care whether there's anything we can do to help the overall functioning of our relationship. Living a haphazard, noncaring life would drive a wedge between us, perhaps even destroy our relationship altogether.

Therefore, we put a lot of emphasis on caring. We find caring truly does recharge our relationship. When you genuinely care about someone, you become involved with that person and his or her life. Thus, you have a stake in that person's life.

Caring Is An Investment

The idea of caring means that you make a calculated investment in your partner. Why investment? Because as you invest in caring for your partner, you expect to get an equal amount of caring in return—during the times you really need it. Of course, now we run into trouble. Sometimes you put hours, days, weeks, or months into caring behavior that would earn Olympic gold, only to have absolutely no caring sent back your way. That's tough to take.

It's usually at this point, then, that your caring becomes your codependence. You do all these wonderful things knowing that you will get nothing back in return.

"Oh well," you sigh deeply and melodramatically. "It doesn't really matter whether I get any care. I need to continue providing care to her." It's that buzzword need—translated into how needy you are—that provides the clue that the balance is upset in a relationship where only one of you exhibits care.

How many times have you sent a "care package" to someone you loved? Perhaps you've sent one to a son or daughter off in college, to a relative you know could use some cheering up, or to your parents as a reminder of your love for them. That care package idea started during World War II with the emergence of an organization called C.A.R.E., an acronym for the Cooperative For American Remittance to Everywhere, Inc.

Even if you are in a relationship that seems to be secure and not in need of particular nurturing, you can still send a sort of "Care Package" to the one you love. It's a dandy way to recharge a relationship. Here's how it works. Remember that caring implies filling a need. In this case, it means filling a need for someone else—your lover, your mate, your special partner.

You can do this as a surprise, say once a week. Wouldn't your partner be pleased to find you had taken the time to pack his or her lunch for a change? And what if in that lunch there was a special treat—a favorite candy bar, a nice card, a love note, a little toy like a pin with some sort of funny saying?

The point isn't what you might pack in the lunch, but rather the fact that you cared enough to do it. Isn't that the real grabber in Hallmark Cards' years-old slogan, "When You *Care* (our italics) Enough To Send The Very Best." It's the caring that counts, not the end product of that care.

We often do this with each other, leaving unexpected cards or notes in places where we wouldn't expect to find one. Under the pillows, taped to the steering wheel, and folded into the day planner are some of the places we have used. It's not uncommon for one of us to find a note taped to the bathroom mirror. It may be asking something in the way of a favor, but it also will always include a message that reinforces our love and concern for each other.

Jack is more than likely to find a note sitting beside his coffee cup or on his leather reading chair. Cyn will find notes laid against her tote bag or the blender, or taped to the coffee maker. Because our schedules are so different, the notes are often headlined 11:30 p.m. (Cyn) or 5:30 a.m. (Jack) and contain a short rundown of what we have been working on or doing. Often our notes extend an invitation to meet for lunch.

Aspects of Caring

Caring about one another doesn't just apply to meeting physical needs exclusively. It also applies to putting yourself out for your partner by recognizing the special burdens that he or she might be carrying. A friendly, "Is there anything I can do to help out with your meeting today?" goes a long way in recharging.

You obviously care when your partner is sick. What are the extra chores, for example, that the well partner picks up in addition to his or her own responsibilities? Caring about what happens to your partner every day means reapplying The Golden Rule. If I care about you and you know that, then I can logically assume that you care about me and will not hesitate to show that care.

Too often, we confuse caring with ordinary helping. When you do laundry or cook dinner and it's not on your shared chores list, you help the relationship (and your partner). When you ask your partner if there is something you can do to help take some pressure off as he or she prepares for a major presentation or a difficult meeting, you are caring.

That your partner might ask you to do laundry or cook the evening meal to help is incidental. The fact that you cared enough to be aware of her special pressures is what counts and what helps recharge a relationship. Think of the swelling of love that you have felt when your partner did do something like that. It was a great feeling, wasn't it? You may have thought, "Wow—he really cares about me!"

Your partner will reflect back to you the amount of care you show. Still, don't care on a quid pro quo basis (I'll-do-this-if-you'll-do-that). No. You show care to recharge your relationship and strengthen the overall fiber of it. If caring isn't a strong factor in your relationship, then the relationship probably will not survive in the long run.

The beauty of caring is the feeling that you give yourself and the care package recipient. It may be a pain in the neck (or elsewhere) for you to pack that lunch, pick up that special card, or put aside what you're doing. But the reward for you is your partner's appreciation. A squeeze of the hand with a "Thanks for asking" is really special, isn't it? What about finding a chocolate on your pillow just like in a fancy hotel? A handwritten note that says what you did or offered was appreciated is worth a whole lot more than expensive gifts for demonstrating love and care in a relationship.

Caring: Real or Imitation?

It's easy to become parental in a relationship. When you care for your partner, he or she can take that caring attitude as parental. For you to say, "It's supposed to snow this afternoon, so be sure to take your boots" sounds pretty parental.

To say, "If it snows today as scheduled will you be okay?" is a caring statement that leaves the responsibility for boots, gloves, and umbrellas squarely with your partner. Your partner notices your care. Presented in this way, care does not lend itself to charges of parenting on your part.

How many times have you noticed people leaving one another with the admonition, "Take care?" What does that mean? It means, of course, to take care of oneself—the usual stuff about not getting into an accident or becoming the victim of a drive-by shooting, if possible. We like to think that "take care" is both a warning and a charge to the other person not only to be careful, but also to take the time and energy to promote caring for themselves during the time you are apart. Yet, people toss out this phrase with the same casual attitude that you hear in "Have a nice day" from the checkout cashier.

We have used that phrase so much that it has become meaning- less. If you don't think that's true, try some smart rejoinder to the person who says it. Something like a simple, "No, I won't," and notice the blank stare or the flustered look you get. You can proba- bly change your own attitude and show a little caring if you begin to tell people, "Make it a good day," thus empowering them to do something about their day. The ways you show care and the ways you receive care are practically boundless. In your recharging capacity, caring is one of the most powerful battery cables you can use. Practice showing care and doing caring kinds of things. Demonstrate a whole new side of yourself that even you didn't know was there just waiting to be unleashed on the world.

When two people begin to say "I love you" so much that it loses its meaning and becomes superficial, it's almost as if the real element of care is just waiting to be called upon. How nice to tell your partner not only that you love him but also that you really like and care about him. Unfortunately, we have also been victimized by the use of care at some time or another in relationships. Caring has been used as a powerful, secret weapon against a partner.

For example, the old phrase "If you really cared about me, you'd buy this for me" has gotten more than one lovesick swain into financial difficulty. He overextends himself, believing that he needs to buy something so that he shows care, which, in turn, will undoubtedly cause love to bloom. We don't think so.

Confusing care and love can be dangerous. You certainly care for people who you have no intention of ever loving, even though there is an unspoken sense of love in every caring act performed. When the great California earthquakes of 1993 occurred, people from all over the world responded in a most heartfelt, caring manner. Their care and their dollars, supplies and shelters all spoke of a love for the victims.

The outpouring of care was the important factor, however. The gift was a sense that human beings could reach out to strangers and offer help, even though they had never met and, in all likelihood, never would meet. That's care in all its nurturing power. You can use that same power. In fact, it's absolutely essential that you do use that power to recharge your own relationship.

You show care, offer care, and use care not with any visible reward in sight, but with an overwhelming desire to demonstrate that you are in tune with your partner's concerns about daily life. It can be so much fun to just think up creative ways (we've included some in the Passion Points) for you to demonstrate the caring side of you in your relationship.

We know on more than one occasion that the chocolate left on the partner's pillow produced unexpected responses, making the act of caring even more of a positive source of recharge. And not just for one night, either!

Passion Points

1. **Care Extensions.** Each of you make a list of things you like that represent caring to you. We suggest you set up two or three columns or categories on a sheet of paper, such as:

Things	Actions	Food

Use a separate food column if there are several particular foods that represent caring to you. Cyn's comfort food list includes Campbell's canned chicken noodle soup, Stouffers frozen macaroni and cheese (brand names can be essential), and grilled cheese sandwiches. Cyn's mom is a very good cook, but she did not like to cook much when Cyn was growing up. Her peanut butter cookies were a real treat that represented caring. Warm, chewy peanut butter cookies are now on the caring list. No other cookie makes this particular list. Look for things, actions, or foods that tell you when someone gives them, does them, or feeds them to you that he or she cares about you.

Examples of "Things" might be bubble bath, a particular aftershave, an item to add to a collection. a flower bud, or golf tees or balls. "Actions" could include recording a TV program, breakfast in bed, free and totally uninterrupted time to do something you love to do, a foot or shoulder massage, or hugs at the door when you get home.

When you complete your lists, keep one copy for yourself and exchange a second copy with your partner. Ask for clarification from your partner of any unclear items on his or her list. Keep both lists with you at all times in your billfold, time planner, or handbag.

Now you have a list that makes it easy to pick up a treat for your mate at the grocery store or while running errands, or to do one simple action on his or her list. Make it a practice to treat your partner to a little caring treat at least twice a week. These are in addition to the bigger gifts or activities like a special dinner out, a piece of jewelry, and so on. The continual smaller caring gifts are the ones that build the feelings that you care and are cared for.

Train yourself to listen to your partner, too, as she mentions additional things that you do or say that make her feel cared for or that she especially appreciates. Add those to your copy of her list regularly. This is especially effective because you not only demonstrate that you care, but also that you listen and are attentive to your partner's needs.

Don't forget to treat yourself, too. When you've had a rough day, do something or get something on your list. When you've done something wonderful, remember to reward yourself.

2.   **Five-to-One Basic Daily Warmup**. A rule of thumb to consider is that marriages that last tend to have five positives for every negative. So if one of you criticizes the other, there should be five positive statements or actions to offset the criticism. Apparently it doesn't matter which of you consciously or unconsciously offers the offsetting positives, as long as the overall ratio for the relationship averages five to one for positive to negative input.

Since you've been diligently doing the earlier exercise listing ten things you like about your partner (right?), let's go one step further.

Each day, call your partner and share one of the things on your list that day or something else positive that comes to mind. Give a little thought or attention to timing. For instance, if your wife has a big meeting to chair in the morning and she's a nervous wreck, leave a message on her voice mail: I just called to tell you I love you. I know you were nervous about this meeting, and I just want you to know that no matter how it turns out I really admire your guts. Then you can bring home a treat from her list—her favorite ice cream, a rose, or something for dinner that you don't have to cook.

If you both do this, obviously you'll be on the phone or leaving messages at least twice a day. If this is a problem with your job(s), then write notes and tuck them in pockets, handbags, briefcases, car seats, lunches. Clip a cartoon or a quote you know your partner will appreciate.

3. **Fetal Curls.** You must be able to care for yourself before you can be very effective at caring for someone else or allowing them to care for you.

At least once a month, preferably every two weeks, do something really unproductive but totally luxurious for yourself. Get some coffee and a roll, crawl back into bed and read a novel or work crosswords for an hour. Take a snack to bed early and watch the football game. Get a massage if you don't usually, or ask your partner to give you one.

You work hard, and you deserve to be pampered. Treat yourself as deserving of care.

9 Sharing: Talking on a Feeling Level

J ack has a favorite description of people who first come into therapy. Before they get into the idea of disclosing their innermost secrets and really working hard to make changes as individuals and couples, they just talk to one another—maybe.

But as soon as they are well into the therapy process they begin to use the word sharing in place of talking when they describe what they do in their relationship. So just what is the difference between talking and sharing?

We use a very simple formula. When two people are exchanging information, gossip, factual data, or casual inquiries ("How are you feeling today?"), they are talking. When they begin to speak of feelings, then they begin the process of sharing. So, for our purposes in this book, let's stick to that formula: When you talk on a feeling level then you are sharing.

What makes sharing such a big deal? In the process of recharging your relationship you have to do things differently. Now, how many times have we already said that in this book? We will keep saying it, too, until the idea is so firmly engraved into your brain that change and the idea of change becomes second nature.

Levels of Communication

So, it's important in a recharging relationship to begin the process of sharing—talking on a feeling level. In order to talk on a feeling level, you must first identify the levels on which you have been talking. There is the most unfeeling level that, unfortunately, too many couples not only start with but also stay with. This is the "Hi-how-was-your-day-what's-for-dinner?" level. Guilty of that? Probably. It's the most uncaring of all the levels of talk. It requires little more than a perfunctory "Okay-how-was-your-day?" that pretty much ends that who exchange.

The next level of talk between couples probably takes place on an "I-heard-on-the-way-home-it-might-snow level." This level revolves around the simple exchange of information and hardly requires much feeling to respond with, "Thanks for warning me. I need to check my antifreeze." That's all. There's no emotion, no verve or vitality—just a simple exchange of information.

The next level in your conversational life is built on gossip or third-party information. It is the Did-you-hear-what-Sally-said-about-Harry? level. This third party level gets a little closer to talking on a feeling level because one or both of the talking partners must add some commentary to whatever the gossip has evoked. In other words, some response of a feeling nature is generally given such as, "Yeah, Harry told me and he also said it wasn't true. And I believe Harry."

So there we have at least the beginnings of sharing because we have some emotions beginning to creep into the conversation. It's pretty easy to slip right on into the next level of talk when you might go a little deeper with, "What makes you always have to take Harry's side of an argument?" Here, there is a clear challenge to probe the partner's feeling levels as the reply might indicate with, "Over the years I've never known Harry to lie. I just feel he's a victim with Sally." Well, paydirt! Your partner has had to take the plunge and actually express a feeling, so now your conversation can begin to be sharing; that is, talking on a feeling level.

Listening

It's important that when someone tells you how they feel about something, your only job is to listen to how they feel and to acknowledge the feeling. You absolutely do not have to do anything about the feeling. Once someone tells you how they feel, it's only necessary for you to allow them to express that feeling.

Responses made to an "I feel" statement are responses that will be on a sharing basis. You will be dealing with one another on a feeling level. Here's a wonderful recipe to help you with creative listening and put you on a feeling level with your partner. It will lead to a new level of sharing.

The author of this is unknown, and you have probably seen it before, but we want you to have it again:

LISTEN

When I ask you to listen to me
and you start giving me advice, you have not done what I
asked.
When I ask you to listen to me
and you begin to tell me why I shouldn't feel that way,
you are trampling on my feelings.
When I ask you to listen to me
and you feel you have to do something to solve my problem,
you have failed me, strange as that may seem.
Listen! All that I asked was that you listen—not talk, or do—
Just hear me . . . .

There is more to that poem, but we just wanted you to have a flavor of what it takes to get to the feeling and sharing level of conversation. We are perfectly aware that there are going to be great objections to trying this. Most of you will complain, rightly perhaps, that you are lucky to even get a grunt of a response from your partner, much less get to a sharing level of talk.

However, that is one of the things that may have kept you stuck in your relationship. It is one of the factors that is missing in the recharging process and one of the important elements that you need to change. You bring about sharing on a feeling level by frankly challenging what makes things so scary for you and your partner that you can't possibly explore the feelings involved.

Rules for Sharing

We suggest you follow these basic rules for sharing, which we have labeled "The Three A's": Acknowledge, Admit, Activate. Here's how they go:

1. Acknowledge that it sounds really difficult for your partner to talk about this, whatever it is.
2. Admit that it's equally difficult for you.
3. Activate the conversation by going first with your feelings.

This gives you the recipe for getting and keeping the conversation on a feeling, sharing level. When you and your partner are openly vulnerable to exposing feelings—that is, the way that whatever is being said or talked about will ultimately affect you—then you are beginning to share.

Sharing is such an important part of our daily lives in almost all other ways, but not quite so in the feelings department. From the time we are little kids, we are admonished to "share that cookie" or "let your friend play with the dolls, too."

We grow up believing that it's okay to share. In fact, it's almost a prerequisite of normal life that we share. Appeals of the Thanksgiving and Christmas holidays are built around sharing. We also share our goods and our prayers and helpful support with disaster victims, and we share canned goods and clothes for the homeless.

Sharing and Vulnerability

But when it comes to sharing our most intimate thoughts—our dreams, hopes, aspirations and our fears—well, then we are riding a horse of a different color. In a relationship, the reason that we are loathe to talk on a feeling level and thus share is because we feel very vulnerable. In the 1994 suspense movie *The Good Son*, we see Macaulay Culkin, normally cast as the defender hero of the *Home Alone* sagas, now representing an eerie, disturbed kid flirting with death ideas. He challenges his cousin as they are about to climb a very tall tree to reach a tree house.

"Are you afraid of heights?" asks Culkin.

"No," responds his cousin, but the camera tells us that he is clearly terrified of the climb ahead of him. He makes the climb—vulnerable to his fear, but not wanting that vulnerability to be another Achilles' heel in his relationship with Culkin.

When two people are afraid of a challenge, often that challenge is to simply share their feelings. Those feelings may expose a raw nerve, bring up unpleasantness, or reopen old wounds that were healing. It's always safe to just talk, but it's often dangerous to consider sharing on a feeling level.

What makes this danger so threatening? When we talk on a feeling level, we really get right down to the basic issues that two people may have with each other. When we were working on this book, Cyn became worried that our own relationship needed recharging because we were both working so hard on projects that we weren't taking time to nurture the relationship.

So it was necessary to do two things:

1. We had to share on a feeling level what we both thought was happening at the moment. Namely, we were breaking one of our own best rules, which is to always keep nurturing our relationship.

2. We needed to take a break. We needed an action plan that meant we shut down the computers and the notebooks full of material and treated ourselves to a Saturday afternoon movie and dinner afterward.

All of that sounds simple enough, and it was. The point is that it never would have happened if we were not able to communicate on a feeling level and share how we felt about getting so involved that we let our priorities slip into second place. Merely saying "I want to go to a movie" wasn't going to get us to a feeling level.

But sharing the words, "I feel as if we are not spending any quality time together lately," evokes a call to action. The second step, however, was to reply to that feeling statement with, "What's making you feel that way?" (Jack)

"We haven't really done anything for us except meet for lunch since we got into the writing phase of the book." (Cyn)

"What do you think of knocking off and grabbing dinner and a movie?" (Jack)

"Sounds like just what we need to do a little recharging." (Cyn)

"How will we make up the time?" (Jack)

"I'll work tonight on the laptop at home. Can you write anytime tomorrow?" (Cyn)

"Sure. I can find two to three hours without a problem."

And so it went, hammering out an agreement and still being able to deal with how we were feeling, or at least how one of us was feeling. And that's another important point about sharing. Often, when one of the partners can share how he feels, the other partner can become aware of her own feelings, which might have just been lying dormant beneath the surface.

But when the one partner can allow himself to be vulnerable and share a true feeling, then it's okay for the other partner to be equally open and sharing and also risk vulnerability. The risk here was in having an argument occur. When Cyn shared her feeling that we were not giving priority (quality time) to our own relationship, she faced the risk of being told "Nonsense!" or some other put-down remark that would have utterly invalidated her feelings.

She chose to share the feeling, believing rightly that what she was feeling could mirror what Jack was feeling but not expressing.

Let's examine another way that sharing can be so much more dynamic to recharging a relationship. Let's talk about sex.

Sex and Sharing

When two people are not sexually active for awhile and tension builds, usually they will say something to the effect of "we need to talk." However, couples will not talk about the issue but invariably will begin to tell each other what he or she is not doing, thus preventing them from having sex. That's what happens when just talk is involved.

In sharing, a couple can get to the feeling level as rapidly as possible by one person saying something like, "I feel that we are not being very intimate lately. What do you think that's all about?"

Now there is a direct request for comment on a feeling expressed by one of the partners. In sharing the feeling (lack of intimacy) the partner is saying, "Tell me on a feeling level what you think is going on with us." The ability to share the feelings means neither partner has to take the blame for what is happening, but rather share the recognition that there is a problem with their intimacy.

Both partners can then continue to talk and listen on a feeling level, sharing what they believe can be done to arrive at a solution. Once again, as in all conversations between the two of you, the idea is to find a solution, not to have one of you right and one of you wrong.

Passion Points

1. **Share Pair Presses.** We think it's important to address a myth that there is some magical way that communication or sharing should take place. We have been presenting guidelines and tools for more effective communication. However, if you have some expectation or idealized picture of how effective communication must be, you're doomed to disappointment.

You may be a very communicative, sharing person with a partner who has trouble getting in touch with feelings, let alone sharing them. Assuming you both want to improve your relationship, as we assume throughout this book, then it is very important you both give up your idealized expectations.

Why? Your less verbal partner may have to draw on every reserve of courage and take what for him or her is a huge risk to make that initial "I feel . . ." statement. It doesn't matter why it's difficult, it simply matters that it is. If you expect suddenly to have wonderfully meaningful exchanges, your partner's first attempts may seem inadequate.

The truth is quite the contrary. Any first efforts at change from either person are admirable and deserving of recognition. You both may feel you fail at first. Good! You learned what doesn't work for you or what you need to work on a little harder.

Building a passionately positive, enduring relationship requires no less investment of time, effort, and continuing education than your career or raising your children. In fact, your relationship can be the foundation supporting everything else you do. You do not want to live in a house or apartment built with cheap materials and a "who cares" work ethic.

So you are investing in your foundation. Your assignment is to begin learning how to construct a quality supporting structure. Every day, take a few minutes to share. Begin simply. Share how you feel about your day. Just one feeling each if that's all you can manage at first. We suggest you hold hands or sit close to each other during this time.

The second part of the assignment is for the listening partner to encourage and praise the sharing partner, no matter what he or she shares. This is not drill time. Initially we suggest you share something not directly related to your partner unless it's a positive feeling. Your job as the listener is to make sure your partner has a safe place to say anything, however inadequately, and receive back from you only acceptance.

2. **Soul Touches.** If we haven't mentioned this before, we will now. We strongly encourage you to keep a journal to record the changes and your feelings about those changes as you progress through these exercises. However, for this exercise, you can use a notepad, tape recorder, or anything else that works for you with your schedule.

It's difficult to share feelings if you don't know what your feelings are. Even those of us who usually are aware of our feelings can lose track of them through work, projects, or other pressures. Some of us never really learned how to recognize feelings, or we learned that some were unacceptable and called them by other names. You may identify anger as hurt, for example, if anger wasn't acceptable in your family when you were growing up.

Again, take a moment during your day to check your feelings. Stop what you're doing, take a deep breath, close your eyes (unless you're driving), and ask yourself what you're feeling. Frustrated? Upset? Angry? Elated? Excited? Nervous? Anxious? Relieved? Just jot down what you're feeling or briefly dictate what you're feeling into your recorder.

If you can spend more time, ask yourself what is causing that feeling. Did you argue with your boss and feel you didn't state your position very well, so you feel angry or frustrated—possibly stupid or inadequate? Did you just deliver the best presentation of your life, and now you feel elated and powerful?

Feelings don't have to be logical. Don't judge your feelings during this exercise. Simply acknowledge them, and be curious about them. You are not your feelings. Feelings have precisely the power and importance you give to them. On the other hand, if you don't take the time to stay in touch with your feelings, they can leach your power of choice before you even realize it's gone.

So, note your feelings. Observe and be curious about them. Don't judge them. Do this every day.

3. **Alternative Approaches a Deux**. Even if you don't usually have problems with sharing, try something different just for fun. If you do have difficulty sharing, take this opportunity to explore ideas about how sharing could work for you.

Try sharing feelings on your computer, or set aside a notepad for this purpose. Don't talk. Just take turns writing or typing what you're feeling. You'll probably be more brief and to the point. And if you're emotionally charged, you'll be a little more careful about what you say and how you're saying it.

If writing isn't your forté, try using a tape recorder in the same way. This has an added advantage if sharing feelings is difficult. It allows you to practice in private. You have the experience of saying your feelings aloud, without performance anxiety, yet knowing that your communication will be heard.

For fun, get some sidewalk chalk and write feeling statements in your garage, on the back porch, on the sidewalk in front of your house, or someplace else relatively private. (You'll probably want to wash up after the sharing is complete, although positive feelings you might want to leave.)

Another alternative is to use a white board or chalkboard to share. Be creative. Draw thunderclouds over your "I feel upset," or rainbows around "I'm happy."

The point is to make sharing feelings fun, entertaining, intimate, and effective. If speaking is difficult, keep trying alternatives to get started.

10 Trust: Life's Great Cement

"**O**h, we have an absolutely wonderful relationship . . . if only . . . ."

"If only what?"

"If only I felt I could really trust him."

Oh sure. It's a great relationship as we eavesdrop on two friends trying to convince one another how solid their relationships are. When that word trust gets thrown about, it's like Thor, the thundering ancient god, hurling thunderbolts down from Mount Olympus.

We talk about trust; we ask for trust; we even demand trust. But it's such a fragile thing that one accident on the romance track can derail the entire relationship. When someone questions whether she can trust, she will always question. She also will probably never let go of the responsibility for trust in the relationship.

Look at it this way. We are asking you to examine the very real possibility that you take ownership of your partner's behavior. When you say, "I wonder if I can trust . . ." you make yourself responsible for that trust remaining intact. We will offer you a different way to look at the subject. Thus, you can recharge a part of your relationship that is always subject to your suspicious fear that trust is being broken.

If Trust Is Broken

So let's start with a very obvious example—that old bugaboo, the affair. We have already told you that many couples will not withstand the disclosure of an affair, no matter what help they get. Jack reinforces his clients by reminding them that an affair is never the issue. An affair is rather a symptom of what has or has not been happening in the primary relationship to allow the affair to get started in the first place.

Nevertheless, let's say that it has happened in your relationship. You have moved beyond it, you think. You have worked through the anger, the hurt, the urge to kill, and all the other passions that are very naturally aroused when such betrayal takes place. So now you are left with the question haunting your mind, "Can I, will I, ever trust him or her again?"

The pre-recharge method had you taking all the responsibility for making sure that your partner always checks in with you, always calls to tell you exactly where and with whom he or she is. You are the official watchdog, police person, conscience, moralist, and so on. You have taken on the entire responsibility for whether or not trust is kept.

In our recharge method, you are officially freed from that responsibility. Turn in your whistle, get out of uniform, and hand in your badges, binoculars, hidden cameras, and paid-by-the-hour private investigators. You're out of work in the trust department. And, we might add, what a wonderful feeling of relief that is.

"But wait a minute," you say. "If I'm not going to guard the trust in this relationship, then who is?"

Your partner is. Plain and simple, it is your partner who first broke the trust (we will assume), and so he or she will now be in total charge of the new trust department in your relationship bank. Here's how it works.

Trust Accounts and the Relationship Bank

Consider that the two of you opened up a trust account in this relationship bank. You each contributed an emotional sum in the form of the energies expended to make the relationship work. That account was growing stronger each day you have been together, earning a kind of wonderful interest that was compounded with new and alluring interest growing between the two of you.

Suddenly, possibly without warning, one of you made a huge withdrawal from the trust account without telling the other partner. You had an affair. The length of the affair, the intensity, who it was—any of the grim and gruesome lovenest details—don't matter in the long run. What does matter is that the trust account was near-ly bankrupted by the disclosure of this breach in the relationship.

Well, you went through all the usual stuff, didn't you? "What the hell is wrong with me that this could happen?" is a typical remark. You probably have taken ownership of what went wrong. Call it codependency if that helps you get the point.

So, trust has been broken. The bank account is nearly empty. We say nearly because you don't totally bankrupt the account because you feel responsible for a piece of this action. For whatev-er reason, the question of trust between you and your partner looms larger and larger after disclosure of the affair.

Every time he or she is out later than usual, or you find some small tear in the fabric of a story, the trust account seems to have a near-zero balance. You've got the picture. Here's the new, recharg-ing part. Instead of you taking on the responsibility for the trust account, what's wrong with making your partner the responsible trustee?

Here's how that works. After the disclosure of the affair (since that's the example we're using), you probably decided you wanted to stay in the relationship. Promises were given, safeguards were offered, and some kind of truce negotiated between you that allowed the relationship another chance.

However (and this is a BIG however), you now take the new, recharging way. You make sure your partner totally understands the consequences of an affair if it happens again. Are you prepared to leave without any more discussion? Do you hightail it to the divorce court? Does it cost the partner something more tangible than the relationship?

No matter what the consequence, the partner must clearly understand that you will take whatever action you decided if trust is ever again broken. And you write the word TRUST on a piece of paper, hand it to your partner, and say, "This is the new deposit in our trust account for our relationship. You carry it with you and understand that only you will either add to or withdraw from the deposit."

Use your own words, but you get the idea. Make the partner take the written word TRUST, put it in a billfold or purse, and always have it with him or her. What this does is twofold: (1) It gives a very clear message that you are not the person responsible for breaking the trust; (2) It highlights your partner's power to determine whether your consequences (leaving, divorce, etc.) will ever be enacted.

This is a powerful tool for recharging your relationship. You don't have to ask all those stupid questions anymore about "Where have you been?" or "Who were you with?" If your partner is somewhere, doing something with someone that shouldn't be being done, then he or she is risking bankrupting the trust account of your relationship.

There is a great freedom in releasing yourself from the responsibility of managing the trust account. If it was your partner who emptied it in the first place, then it is your partner who will be anxious to rebuild the account by doing and saying what is necessary to help you regain trust in him or her.

If your partner says, "I'll be home by 9:00 and I'll be at the following number until then," he or she is making a big deposit to the trust account. You can check up on the story. Or, you can help build the trust account by believing your partner, knowing that your mate is fully responsible for the growth of the trust account. To bankrupt it is to face your consequences.

Don't confuse trusting with lying, either. They are two different tracks that partners can run on, and you must always use trust as a building block in recharging your relationship. If your husband or wife has frequent business lunches with members of the opposite sex, you trust that they are for business. If they are for pleasure, then you have a right to ask that you come along. That's how trust gets built.

If your partner says he or she is spending money for a particular item, you have every right to trust that is how the money will be used. If you open your joint check register and find the money was spent on something else, then confront your partner. If he or she denies it, then look to lying. This has nothing to do with trust. Trust comes the next time your partner asks for money and you wonder if it will be used as requested.

Trust and the Dual-Career Couple

In today's world where so many people are two-career couples, trust is an even more important cement than ever. Now, people are expected to travel alone or with people of the opposite sex. If people want to compete for top jobs, they perform top-level tasks. Travel, alone or with other employees, is part of the job.

Trust is a traveling companion with them. One couple we know had a problem with this. In her previous relationship, Claire could never get her live-in companion to leave the name or number of the hotel where he would be staying in another city. His excuse was always that he needed to be flexible and wasn't sure if he would make that particular city when he thought he would.

If he said he was going to Boston, he might call from Chicago instead. He'd tell Claire that he couldn't conclude his business in

Chicago in time to catch his flight to Boston, so he would stay over and go on to Boston the next day. This went on until Claire found a note with the name of a hotel in Boston, called the hotel, and asked them to ring his room. Sure enough, he was there and had been there all along.

She confronted him upon his return and discovered that he was seeing his ex-wife in Boston. Furthermore, he had slept with her. Broken, hurt, and angry, Claire promptly gathered her things and moved out. Now, however, she has a real trust issue with the man she is with. Would Paul pull the same kind of stunts since he also traveled?

Indeed not. Our hero came through like the champion he is. When Paul went out of town, he called Claire as soon as he checked in. He gave her the number of the hotel and the number of his room. He told her when he was going to dinner and that he would call her to say goodnight when he got back to his room.

These are all simple things, but the more Paul used them, the more Claire's trust account grew strong and secure. A small investment of time and longer-distance phone expense was more than offset by the interest paid from that trust account. It was unlikely that Paul was up to no good. He loves Claire and wants the trust account always to be secure. So he does things that help build up that account.

Claire told us that it was wonderful not to worry about her man's traveling the way she had in her previous relationship. She admitted she had been frightened that this same behavior would be repeated in her new relationship, and she would once again be left asking herself, "What did I do to deserve this again?"

This is another example of doing whatever it takes to get rid of the old tapes and replace them with new, trusting tapes that nurture and recharge a relationship. Trust accounts can become so strong that they are the very lifeline of your relationship that cement it together.

"Just Trust Me"

The old movie dialog, "Don't worry, darling . . . just trust me," has been misused a lot over the years. We know there are times you think you will just absolutely lose it if someone asks you to trust them again. Husbands and wives of alcoholics, cocaine snorters, or shoplifters have heard, "Trust me! This won't happen again, I assure you!" too many times. Well, we know sometimes how far that kind of trust goes. When the word trust is bandied about freely and with little or no regard to what it means between two people, then it really does lose its punch.

The pilot who says, "We're expecting a smooth ride this morning, folks," is asking you to trust his or her expertise at the controls of a manmade object hurtling through the atmosphere at thirty-five thousand feet at six hundred-fifty miles per hour. And what choice do you have if you want to fly? So you trust the pilot explicitly with your life. You trust that he or she is properly and expertly skilled to do what needs to be done, and you have paid hard-earned money to get you where you want to go quickly and safely.

You trust your parish priest, pastor, rabbi, or spiritual advisor. When your therapist, doctor, or dentist speaks to you as a professional authority, you trust their words.

How many times have you faced a barrage of questions and stacks of papers awaiting your signature from lawyers, accountants, and financial advisors? "Just sign here where you see the 'X'," they say. You say, "God, I can't understand all this stuff, Max. I just have to trust that you know this is the right thing." And Max replies, "Trust me, John, that's what you pay me for."

Well, maybe. You have to admit that humans put an awful lot of blind trust in our fellow travelers through this life. Winning political candidates put their assets into blind trusts and rely on someone else to manage their affairs without their knowledge. That way, no hint of impropriety will befall the candidate while he or she holds public office. Thus, we have presidents and legislators eagerly showing the media that if they have holdings in a particular defense contractor's company, they don't personally have knowledge of that holding because they set up a blind trust account when elected to office.

In your relationship, you also set up a kind of blind trust. You make a large investment in your relationship and assume that your partner will nurture that investment and grow with you to help make your relationship strong, powerful, and exciting. Relationships should also be rewarding. Of course, the element of trust plays a very large part in that growth.

By recharging your relationship, we are asking you to make a major change in how you have viewed trust. We are asking you to set up this trust account with your partner, each of you with equal responsibility for its growth, maturity, and bounty. Or, you share equally in the disaster of bankrupting this account by selfish, deceitful, and hurtful behaviors.

We know one thing: Every couple must talk about and understand the importance of trust in their relationship. They must also be willing to explore the new ways that a broken trust account can be rebuilt. Systems of checks and balances need to be established so they will never again look at a trust account sheet that shows a zero balance.

Passion Point

1. **Working Out With Runs and Bolts.** This is a tough exercise, so we'll have just one Passion Point this chapter.

   Choose an issue of trust between you. It doesn't have to be serious, but if you have something serious use it.

   For the sake of simplicity, we'll call the partner who broke the trust Partner Who Runs from Anger and the other Partner Throwing Lightning Bolts—"Runs" and "Bolts" for short.

The first step is to have a Ten-Minute Drill around the issue, with the purpose of arriving at a new agreement about how trust will be reestablished. Bolts outlines the specific consequences if the action in question is repeated. Runs promises what he or she will do to ensure Bolts will not have to worry in the future. Bolts writes the word "trust" on a piece of paper and gives it to Runs.

Each partner now has individual assignments.

RUNS: Your first action is to put the Trust Deposit in a safe place, preferably a place where you will see it often.

Whatever you have promised, you must absolutely do it without fail. If you promised to call before you leave your office, then you must do that every single time. Keeping that promise should be the most important thing on your agenda. You will not be doing so just for your partner, although your commitment to the quality and growth of your relationship will make keeping your word important for that reason. Do this for yourself more than anyone else. You are the one who will benefit incredibly from the personal growth in keeping your word absolutely, with no exceptions.

You have no option about keeping your promise if you want to recharge, even survive, your relationship. Trust is priceless in a relationship, and you are responsible for adding interest to that trust deposit your partner gave you.

BOLTS: You have now given your Trust Deposit to your mate, and your assignment is just as difficult as Runs'. You are to completely let go of the Trust Account. You have clearly stated the consequences in the Ten-Minute Drill if your partner bankrupts the account. You have to be fully prepared to follow through with those consequences if that happens. Otherwise, your job is to forget about the whole situation.

How can you do this? Realistically speaking, you probably can't forget for awhile. However, remember that if you treat someone as if he or she can't be trusted, even while trying to be trustworthy, eventually that person will begin to wonder, understandably, about the point of changing.

The best procedure for Bolts is to get busy taking care of yourself and your responsibilities. Do some serious work on your self-image, self-esteem, and personal growth. Many books, articles, and therapists are available to help you with this task. Find something you've wanted to do or try and start doing it. Learn a new skill or hobby. Your job is to be someone no one in his or her right mind would want to betray or disappoint. You may already be such a person, but keep working to fine-tune yourself. After all, at least for some period of time, you were someone who was betrayed. This isn't about Runs now; it is strictly about you.

You know what you want to do. Whatever you do to keep your mind occupied, do not check up on your partner. He or she should be doing everything promised to reestablish trust. Your role is to behave as if the trust is already reestablished and to recognize and reward the changes resulting from your partner's efforts.

If you try to control your partner in any way, you will never know if you can trust him or her again. Before you can trust again, you have to risk learning that your partner can't be trusted. Isn't that better than living in constant fear and worry? The other side of the risk is that you'll learn that your partner can be trusted. And that's definitely worth taking the risk.

11

Touching:
Hugs and Kisses
without Sex

Wouldn't you just love to think that the special person in your life would be happy just to hold you and give you a "warm fuzzy" without attempting to jump your bones? Are we kidding? Well, maybe not.

We believe that when a couple learns the value of touching, hugging, and kissing without the expected sexual payoff, real recharging begins. Unfortunately, people are often afraid to touch one another, even relatives and friends. Sadly (we believe), the politically correct attitude and the heightened awareness of sexual harassment in the workplace makes us pretty cautious about the simple act of giving someone a warm fuzzy in the form of a hug.

Look around you the next time you're at the airport in your city. How many people hug when greeting arrivals from the concourse? How many times do you see men hugging? More often you will observe women hugging each other, yet it seems to be a dying form of greeting. There is too much fear the hug will be taken in the wrong, sexually covert manner, even though it may be a best friend from high school or college who you are genuinely glad to see.

The idea of exchanging a hug or kiss without it leading to sex is certainly not new. Most of the gurus of self-help, like the esteemed Leo Buscaglia, have espoused the hug for years. We don't believe you can ever undo a true "Leo fan." Nor do we want to. Giving a hug in a relationship is one of the most tender and supportive acts that two people can bestow upon one another. It pains us to see fathers shaking hands with grown sons instead of embracing. It is sad to see a mother offer only her cheek to a daughter when you just know the daughter yearns for more warmth and expression of a silent "I love you" than she is getting.

We make fun of the French as the world's "premier embracers," but you can't discount the friendly bear hug that a Russian bestows upon you. Or how about the warm, almost rib-cracking hug of an Italian or Spanish friend or acquaintance? So what makes it so difficult for couples who share intimate surroundings of daily life— undressing in the same room and sharing a bed, bath, and intimacies of birthing and dying—to share a hug?

Space Invasion

What is happening is an invasion—a real, honest-to-God invasion. Your space is being invaded when a hug is coming your way. What's so bad about that? Well, only that you feel suddenly vulnerable. Therefore, the safety net that you carry around all the time for emotional protection gets a big tear.

The hugger has violated your airspace, so to speak, and you are ready to shoot down the intruder. How many times after a really hard-on-both-of-you fight, has there been an opportunity to kiss and make up? This usually will be proffered by the one who is anxious to keep the fight from spoiling the remainder of the day, night, or weekend. How hard has it been to have your offer accepted if you suggested making up?

What has prevented you or your partner from walking across that imaginary line drawn in the sand and making the first move toward a hug and kiss that would begin the reconciliation? It's pride. Oh, yes, the downfall of so many relationships rears its ugly head again. You'll be damned if you are going to be the one who hugs first.

Well, pride is not going to recharge your relationship. Hugs won't do it alone either, but they sure will help pave the way. Let's go back to that imaginary line drawn in the sand. The fight is over. Hopefully you have used the Rules of Fair Fighting outlined earlier, and there is a win-win ending.

Affection Does Not Equal Sex

So, how come you still can't bring yourself to cross the line and give the hug? If you are the female, your reluctance may be based on your experience that your male partner just doesn't know how to gives hugs and kisses without it leading to a romp on the bed, on the floor, wherever. If he gets within ten feet of touching you, you are automatically fearful of what can follow.

This is something that can be changed and indeed needs to be changed if you are serious about the benefits of touching one another without it leading to sex. It requires your being willing to talk with your partner about several things:

1. How important hugs and kisses are to you.
2. How you want hugs but don't want sex (right then).
3. How you want to give hugs and kisses freely.

Now that's not such a tall order to fill. If the two of you will look at that simple list, you can be on the way to discovering what has made it difficult for those things to happen in the past. People are not comfortable with the idea of touching one another in the first place. Touching each other very likely was a part of your premarital or prerelationship sexual advances. From the beginning of your relationship there was a physical attraction, obviously, and perhaps the heat of the moment was exacerbated by touching one another with the promise of more intimate and more sexual behavior to come. You may also have been a couple for whom sex occurred from the very first date or occasion when you were alone, and therefore you never really explored the possibilities of nonsexual touching. Hugging and sensory improvements, such as massages, back rubs, muscle kneading, and other nongenital stimulations, can do so much to charge and recharge your relationship.

We believe there is absolutely nothing to compare to the wonderful feeling of giving a good back rub or message, complete with warm baby oil or scented oils. Or, take an hour or more to touch each other in a loving, sensual (not sexual), and caring way.

There is no question that erotic feelings are spurred by the feel of your hands on your partner's naked body. The music playing, the candles burning, the warm oil making you feel incredibly relaxed as your partner's hands help remove the stresses of the day can be arousing. But how more wonderful it feels to just give that message and not have to have anything (in the form of sex) in return. At least for the moment, it is a way that touching one another can simply offer the support of one human to another and become a way of saying "I care about you, in addition to loving you."

How many times have you wanted to say to your partner, "Just hold me, please?" Think of times when your stress level has been very high, when you've had a personal defeat and you feel so absolutely alone and maybe even frightened. That's when the hugs of your partner mean the most, don't they?

What has made you afraid to ask for those hugs? One of the answers lies in the possibility that you will be rejected. That would hurt almost as much as the things that cause you to ask for the hug in the first place. The specter of rejection has been present in your relationship anyhow, if you are really truthful. There have been times when you have felt passionately motivated to put some moves on your partner, haven't there? Sure, and yet you have held back, sensing that there could be a turndown. You would then feel the sharp blade of rejection, fearful of taking such a risk again.

The Hug Store

So, try our plan for the "hug store" for openers. Here's how it works. When the world seems dark and bleak—when it looks like the "winter of our discontent" will never end—it's time for a visit to the hug store. One of you, looking for reassurance, comfort, and security, asks the partner, "Is the hug store open by any chance?"

That's your opportunity to say, "You bet!" and to embrace the person who is asking. We do this a lot in our relationship, and we're proud to share it with you. Sometimes, leading busy and hectic lives as we do, it seems that we have simply not taken enough time for each other. That's usually when one of us asks about the hug store. Both of us know that our hug store keeps very regular hours, even if there have been some gritchy words between us.

The opportunity for a couple to exchange hugs and experience warm fuzzies is universal. It goes back when we were infants. Being held, comforted, and soothed was what we sought to help us make it through this big, tough world.

Think back to the earliest skinned knees, bruised elbows, or black eyes from schoolyard tussle. Sure, we probably got a lecture, a bandage and disinfectant, an ice pack and a sling, but we really hankered for a hug. An "It'll be okay," coupled with a warm embrace, made us instantly feel that it really would be okay.

This is what makes the hug store such a valuable piece of real estate in the relationship market. A hug, openly asked for and freely given, can be even more powerful than the most intimate of sexual stimulations. When one of us gets so tied up in the business of our professional everyday worlds, it is not uncommon to hear either of us yell from one part of the house where we are working, "Hey, you! By any chance is the hug store open today?"

For a partner to ask for a hug does not mean they are weak, sick, emotionally unable to cope, or any of that stuff. It simply means, "I derive a strength from you when you hug me, and I want that transfusion of your warmth, love, and security that only you can bring me."

Expanding the Safe Zone

Then, of course, we come back to the part about hugs that seems scary, intimidating, and anxiety provoking for a lot of people. Social scientists tell us that human beings have a safe zone of something like eighteen inches. That is, when another human being is "in your face" and violating that eighteen-inch safety zone, you tend to feel threatened.

We like to think of the safe zone as being a little larger. Translating, if you were to stand alone, draw an imaginary circle around your feet that has an eighteen-inch radius, which gives you a thirty-six-inch imaginary circle. When someone steps inside that circle, you are inclined to feel threatened.

What's really happening is that when someone intrudes into that "safe circle," you automatically get an adrenalin rush. The adrenalin is preparing you to flee or fight, to take care of the intruder. Of course, what we're wanting you to do is hug instead of flee or fight. Still, think of the times when you felt a sudden discomfort if someone, particularly a stranger, violated your safe zone. Now think of the times that your partner also has violated that zone, and think of how you felt. How could it be different for you? If your hug store is truly going to be open, then you won't have feelings of panic or anxiety that you have when strangers, quarreling family members, a threatening spouse, or a potential attacker (verbal or physical) alert your system.

We ask you to risk promoting your hugs and kisses without sex to further the idea of recharging your relationship with sensual, not sexual, touching.

Getting and giving hugs is a way that you communicate to your partner in a nonverbal manner. It is one of the things that you can share without fear of running out, or without any danger that they will become obsolete or out of style. Hugs, asked for or freely given, are a way of addressing the importance of your relationship as being a living thing, equally in need of tender loving care as your houseplants and your pets.

Touching

We feel the same way about touching. How nice it is to be able to just hold your partner's hand, stroke the face, or even give a friendly pat on the butt without having it go any further. When was the last time you and your partner were seen holding hands as you walked in the mall, down the aisle at church, or even in the grocery store? Too long, we'll bet. Once again, ask yourself the reason for this fear of touching one another.

In so many cases, there simply hasn't been enough conversation between the two of you to tell one another that you really like to hold hands, or stroll arm in arm, or exchange playful love pats. It's incredible that so many couples are afraid to ask for what they want from their partner.

We stress the fact that touching has too often been linked to having sex. What a shame that the mere act of expressing ourselves to our partners cannot be perceived as affection and as a symbol of commitment and happiness at the mere idea of being together. It requires your constant practice in the art of touching to become comfortable with it and to separate it from a prelude to sex.

In Dr. Irene Kassorla's excellent book, *Nice Girls Do*, one can learn how important touching, massaging, and simple sensory exercises can be to enhancing the relationship between two people. There is a vast chasm of difference between the frantic groping, grasping, lunging and tearing that could accompany the wildest of sexual sessions, and the gentle touching, caressing, feeling, massaging, stroking, and holding patterns of lovemaking.

Think in terms of making love to your partner all the time without actually having to engage in the act of sexual intercourse itself. We're not talking about walking around like "velcro couples"— stuck together and joined at the hip—but rather being a couple committed to the idea of sharing.

The idea of touching is an idea of things to come in more intimate settings, at more appropriate times. Most important is the idea that touching reconnects you and your partner to some of the basic reasons that you are a couple. Our friends have been around us so long and heard about the hug store so much that the idea has spread. They use the idea and like it, and we are amused to hear one of the partners ask, "Is the hug store open yet?" when we are visiting.

Think of the gift of life that comes through touching. Michelangelo's wonderful painting, on the ceiling of the Cistine Chapel in the Basilica of St. Peter in Rome, depicts the hand of God the Creator reaching to touch the hand of Adam, and in touching him, giving him the gift of life.

In Steven Spielberg's touching fantasy, *E.T., The Extra Terrestrial*, who could not be moved at the moment when the alien's long bony fingers make contact for the first time with the wonder-filled human boy who was to become his friend and champion? That simple act of touching said more than any dialog. Recharge the spirit of your relationship by taking the risk of touching again, of hugs and kisses without sex. The electricity that will flow between you is a constant reminder of the energy that this touching helps create between two people who are interested in continuing to grow together, richer, more complete and in harmony.

Passion Points

The exercises for this chapter will likely improve your sex life. However, the common objective during these exercises is to *not* have sex. (Of course, we all know accidents will happen. If you blow it, just do the exercise again later.)

Another objective for this section is to turn ourselves into lovers. Just think—some of the most famous lovers in history and literature had little or no sex with each other.

It is important that both of you agree to at least try to not have every exercise lead to sex. You want to build your capacity for close physical intimacy. Unless both of you are in the mood to make love, you will probably find ways to avoid the exercises and sex rather than risk starting something you don't want to finish. You may discover a couple of things: Maybe sometimes you really want closeness and not sex, and maybe becoming more intimate without sex will greatly enhance your sexual experiences.

1. **The Lover's Warmup.** Both of you pick a week to concentrate, individually, on thinking about all the most romantic, nonsexual episodes you've seen in movies, read about, heard about, or experienced. Focus on pulling together a role model of a lover for yourself. You are not looking for all the things your partner does not do. You are looking for all those things that you can do to practice being a lover.

Some of the actions and characteristics of a lover you notice as you recall those scenes might include:

Attentiveness	Gentle touching or stroking
Lots of eye contact	Humor
Courtesy	Respectful demeanor
Smiling	Sensual (not sexy) attire
Vulnerability	

You'll think of many more characteristics, we're sure, but these are the kinds of things to look for. Jot some of them down as you think of them. Start thinking of ways you can incorporate some of these characteristics and behaviors yourself. For instance, sensual attire can mean wearing a soft, clingy robe before bed instead of the ratty college T-shirt and the sweats with the huge hole in the rear. Gentle touching or stroking can be gently stroking the inside of your partner's elbow while watching television or sharing your feeling about the day.

Start incorporating these characteristics and practicing the behaviors with your mate, and in your own style. Don't try to be someone you're not, but try to become more than you are as a lover—no matter how good you are. Don't try to be "on" all the time, but try to be aware of yourself as a lover all the time.

2. **Total Body Tingle.** Invest in an inexpensive set of body paints or some nontoxic, washable fingerpaints that kids use. Pick up a few inexpensive paint brushes at the crafts store. Usually these stores will have some on sale for around a dollar. You're looking for softness and assorted sizes rather than quality.

Pick a time when you can spend at least a couple of hours alone without interruption. Your plan is to take turns painting each other's bodies. The more paint in more detail on the most body places, the better. You can use eyeliner pencils to draw outlines and paint intricate designs, or paint pictures that particular contours bring to mind.

When you're painting, notice all the little places on your lover's body that you never noticed or paid much attention to. Notice his or her skin texture and the subtle colors of shadows and undertones. Notice where you want to make broad long flowing paint strokes and where you want to make little delicate strokes. Think about how the brush and the paint feels to your partner.

If you're being painted, notice what feels good and what tickles. Notice when you're uncomfortable and what makes you that way. Remember that your partner is focusing on painting, not on the perfection of your body structure. How does it feel to completely relax and surrender to being gently stroked all over? Are you being turned into a giant butterfly or the tattooed lady? Keep relaxing and noticing your feelings and sensations.

When you're finished or have to stop, share a warm bubble bath together and wash all the paint off of each other. Spend at least fifteen minutes in the bath together. Share what really felt good, what parts of your body seemed the most and least sensitive. Since the assignment was to paint everything, you can share what didn't feel good without either of you being concerned about having done something wrong or being critical. It's a great, nonthreatening way to learn your partner's favorite places to be touched, and how.

3. **Intimate Initiatives.** Remember the exercises don't include sex. Three times a day select one of the following:
    *   French kiss for a count of twenty. (Try counting it once or twice, then just estimate the time.)
    *   Share an extended hug—full body, no briefcases, groceries, or other barriers in hand.
    *   Snuggle for five minutes on the sofa or in bed, even if you don't go to bed at the same time. (Remember, there is no sex at these times, so dishes, dinner, or the report can wait for these little bits of time.)
    *   Shower together.
    *   Undress together.
    *   Nap together.

12 Earning Respect

"**I** get no respect," moans America's forlorn funnyman, Rodney Dangerfield.

"If I sleep with you, will you respect me in the morning?" asks the sweet innocent thing in a million pulp novels or B movies.

"I don't know. I just feel that my parents never respected me," the embittered young man says in a therapy session. "When I chose engineering instead of law school, that was it," he adds with a sense of finality. Well, rechargers, is that it? We don't think so. The idea of respect is as important in recharging a relationship as all other factors we are introducing. It may even have a special significance of its own.

When a couple make a commitment to one another, they really are saying, "I respect you and what you are, what you stand for, and what I believe you will contribute to our relationship." When Cyn does something in the way of her creative art work, or Jack turns out something from their workshop that really works, there is an exchange of respect for the partner.

It's almost tinged with a small tweak of envy. "I think you did a great job on those papier maché bowls," gushes Jack. And then he might add, "I'm sure I could learn to do that, but probably never as well as you."

Admiration and Esteem

Respect for one another means ungrudging admiration for each other in all areas of life. It encompasses talents, skills, special abilities, and the way your partner conducts his or her everyday life. *Webster's New World Dictionary* defines *respect* "to feel or show honor or esteem for." But we are also cautioned that respect means "to show *consideration* (our italics) for; avoid intruding upon or interfering with," as in respecting one's privacy.

If you consider the Latin root word, *respectus,* then you have a purer definition: "to look at, look back on, respect." No matter how you define respect, what's important is the way a couple uses respect in their efforts to recharge their relationship. Take privacy, for example. Are you entitled to it? Do you get it? The answers are "yes" and, probably, "no" or "sometimes." What happens with couples that they begin to take ownership over their partner's lives?

We find it extremely detrimental to see how codependency (there's that word again) grows to become total parenting and ownership of all responsibility for the partner's every action. You know the drill and have been through it many times: "Did you remember to pay the utility bill?" "Have you taken out the garbage?" You treat one another as if you function on just half a brain cell. In short, you entirely disrespect the native intelligence that your partner possesses to function very well in your relationship without prompting for every action. It's hard to back off back, unfortunately, because having respect for your partner means to be willing not to adopt a parenting role.

You show very little respect for your partner's ability to pull his or her fair share of the load when you constantly take charge of every damn thing in the relationship. We are all guilty, however, of having done just that. It's a tough habit to break, but you certainly must break it to allow respect to be a functioning part of a recharging relationship.

However, you can give respect on one hand and snatch it away with the other before your partner can relish one moment of it. One of Jack's clients years ago used to do this with consummate skill. When asked how his weekend had been, this man would allow a big smile to cross his face and say, "Real good. I got Gert treed pretty early on Saturday and kept her there most of the weekend."

Translation: This man liked engaging in verbal battles with his wife and respected her ability to dish it back to him as he would often admit by saying things like, "She almost had me once or twice but I rallied late to win." His respect for her verbal jousting was offset by his gloating over "getting her up a tree."

He admitted this was chauvinist behavior, but it was meant and taken by the couple as good fun. People get respect, we're told, by earning it. We could not help but be impressed with the way the late, great stage actor, John Houseman, brought respect to a brokerage house TV commercial. Houseman, who became popular because of his superb portrayal of Professor Kingsley in TV's *Paper Chase*, would close the TV commercial by intoning with deepest gravity, "At Smith Barney we make money the old fashioned way . . . we earn it."

How could one not be overwhelmed by a sense of respect after having that message drummed into us at the best of prime times? Earning respect has been a major goal for emerging Third World countries, hasn't it? We read and hear every day about the battles of protocol that are waged not only at the United Nations but in all gatherings at which more than one nation is represented. The term respect is bandied about more than peace, justice, or equality.

Bestowing and Earning Respect

A head of state's place at an important dinner table has to do with respect. Christ admonishes us to sit "beneath the salt" at table so that "others who are more esteemed" may have the place of honor.

We are made very aware of what lack of respect means from the time we were disciplined as small children. Jack remembers times in a Catholic school cloakroom when a nun would administer the slap on the hand with a ruler for lack of respect. All of us can recall parents thundering, "Listen, young man (woman), I am your mother (father), and you can't talk back to me like that. It's disrespectful."

Feel free to substitute dialog you remember. You get the idea, we're sure, of the importance that respect or lack of it has played in your life.

In a relationship, almost every action that you and your partner take is flavored with respect or lack of it. When an errant partner continues to stay out late and doesn't phone to tell you where he or she is, is this flaunting a lack of respect for you, not to mention possible violation of relationship trust?

What about the way your partner treats you in the company of others? Have you been the subject of humor that you didn't consider funny at all? How many times have you heard so-called macho men refer to their mates, girlfriends, or partners as "the old lady," the "ball and chain," the "little woman," and so on? Have you heard women talk about their "old man," not meaning their father, or use some other derogatory description of their relationship partner? Isn't it a gross lack of respect, and isn't it damaging to the relationship?

When you love someone, you respect them on a number of different levels. You respect them for their abilities in their chosen profession. You respect their abilities as parents, grandparents, or caring uncles or aunts. We hear often of men and women who garner great respect from their partners for their care of animals or plants.

Respect in a recharging relationship is a renewed, continuing acknowledgment of what the skills and practices of your mate mean to the growth of the relationship. When your partner tackles some new skill and becomes proficient at it, don't you respect that accomplishment? What do you feel for a partner who overcomes a tremendous social handicap to move forward better than ever before?

You probably have a new respect for the partner who is able to kick the smoking habit or enters recovery from alcohol or drug abuse. Respect in a recharging relationship is one of those "goodies" that you can use to great advantage for the growth of the relationship.

We have often heard divorced people talk with great impunity about their previous mates, only to cap off a particular point with, "But I sure respect her as the mother of our kids." When you use respect as recharger, you should offer it along with praise.

If your partner's sewing room or workshop project isn't quite what you believed it was going to be, you still praise the accomplishment. Therefore, what is wrong with adding, "I really respect the fact that you tackled this project, even though I know you were hesitant to do it."

The kid who repeatedly tries to make the football team but just doesn't have the natural talent certainly deserves respect for trying. He or she earns that respect. When we watch the Olympics on TV, we cannot help but admire the accomplishments of the world's athletes. How much more respect do you feel for the physically disadvantaged who participate so keenly in Special Olympics?

In your relationship, your partner may make the same dumb mistakes over and over until you think you will probably just lose it and scream. You try to explain, with no results, how your partner's actions drive you up the wall.

Miraculously, the partner starts getting it right. Not only are you relieved and gratified by this change, but you respect the partner for making the change for the betterment of the relationship. Even if you don't say it, you have to feel that his or her changing is a sign of respect for you and the relationship.

We always talk about earning respect as if it were some wage offered for a job well done. In recharging your relationship, respect ought to be a given. It is something you wear like a badge of honor on behalf of the partner and your relationship. Others can give respect, that always seems like something earned, but it may come in funny, different ways.

When Jack's first book, *The Joy of Being Sober*, was published, he went on a 14-city promotional tour. The tour included lectures, book signings, radio and TV appearances, and the usual "hype" promotions. In one city, a man approached Jack and said, "I read your book." That was it. No other comment, no compliment, no criticism, just, "I read your book." The man walked away, leaving Jack quite puzzled as to what that was all about. Finally, the man turned around, came back to the signing table, and offered his hand for Jack to shake.

"I really respect your honesty about your drinking," he said. It didn't matter that Jack never did know what the man thought about the book. He had earned the man's respect as a person.

Cyn continuously was complimented by family members and friends for completing her undergraduate and graduate degrees while maintaining a full-time job and being part of our relationship. In school, she also earned summa cum laude and master's honors. At a reception given in her honor, a woman said to Cyn, "I cannot tell you how much I respect your persistence. I'm not sure I could have done it."

The Main Course

In your recharging mode, think of respect as something that is more than just the topping on the cake. Make it part of the main course. When you are Fair Fighting, for example, learn to say, "I respect your feelings about . . ." or "I have a great respect for your position on that." When you offer respect, you acknowledge the accomplishments your partner has achieved that have already given him or her the right to your respect. Studying chess, bridge, or tennis and then soundly beating opponents at the games earns respect for the time, effort, and talents that the person has corralled to be a winner. When you say to your partner "I respect . . ." you are acknowledging past accomplishments, even if they just happened.

For example, in the course of a discussion or a Fair Fight Drill, your partner may suddenly back off of what seemed like an unreachable position. When that happens, you should acknowledge it with, "I respect that you just changed your outlook on that. I know that's hard to do in the middle of a drill. It makes me feel you really value our relationship."

We posed the question "Will you earn respect?" at the beginning of this chapter. Probably more important to the recharging process is whether you are willing to earn respect and how important having new respect is to you. It doesn't matter whether you are from a titled family or from a dirt-poor background. You can't garner respect if you don't do things in your relationship that throw light on why you should be respected.

You may have heard the old story about the kid complaining because he has to walk to school. The parent responds: "I walked to school every day, both ways, in the dead of winter." The kid usually walks away, mumbling under his breath, "Yeah, and I'll bet it was uphill both ways, too." The kid gets no respect and the parent gets no respect because he didn't address the child's complaint. Instead, the parent forced his own experience to the foreground. Couples do this, too, and it shows a complete lack of respect for the partner and the issue at hand.

Start with Respect

Recharging means starting with respect for each other and for the relationship that you are creating together. The fact that you are interested in recharging means that you respect each other's ability to work through problems and find new and better solutions to things that have kept your relationship stuck in neutral or reverse.

Respect means that you are willing and able to prioritize making your relationship all that it can be, all that you dreamed possible, and even many things you believed impossible. What you respect is the talent and ability that both of you will expend to make this thing work. You respect the fact that your partner will make new efforts and spend more time, even money, because of the desire to keep your relationship on track and to enhance your ability to find the fun again—to "go where no couple has gone before" (forgive us *Star Trek*).

Truthfully, couples are making this commitment all the time. When we talk to them about recharging their relationship, they give a blank look at first, like maybe we've been at the joy juice ourselves. But as we talk to them about the very things we are asking you to do, we see a sparkle come into their eyes, a sense of desire to take some risks, and, most of all, a respect for each other as soon as one of them says, "I'd be interested in recharging our relationship." When respect for one another comes bubbling to the surface, it helps a couple to remember the qualities of the partner that made respect seem present from the beginning.

We salute a military officer or a head of state out of respect for the office more than the person. It is a way of giving recognition to all that the office and rank mean. In his excellent book, *A Hero For Our Time*, Ralph Martin relates the story of Rose Kennedy preparing to deplane the presidential aircraft ahead of her son, John. "No mother," Kennedy said. "The President of the United States will get off first."

Respect. It is there for the office of presidents, for generals, admirals, kings, and even husband, wife, lover, or the significant person in your life.

Try respect on for size and use it frequently as a recharge tool.

Passion Points

1. **Respectfully Yours**. Once again, write each letter of the word respect on a separate line.

> R
> E
> S
> P
> E
> C
> T

For the first part of this exercise, each of you work on your own to write a word or thought beginning with each letter. As you try to think of words that fit the acronym, jot down other words and ideas that come to mind that represent respect to you.

When you've each completed the exercise on your own, compare your responses and the other ideas about what respect means to you. Take turns talking about the reasons for using certain words.

2. **Attitude Adjustment**. Following are three quotes dealing with respect.

"If a person of your intelligence and competence and commitment disagrees with me, then there must be something to your disagreement that I don't understand, and I need to understand it. You have a perspective, a frame of reference I need to look at." (Regarding respect during disagreements, Stephen Covey, *Seven Habits of Highly Successful People*, p. 270)

"As long as people have the same goals, it is not important that they have the same roles. When team members regard each other with mutual respect, differences are utilized and are considered strengths rather than weaknesses." (Stephen Covey, *Principle Centered Leadership*, p. 246)

"Never take another person for granted. You demonstrate respect for other people by never taking them for granted, even when you know you can count on them for support. To assume that you needn't talk with them, listen to their ideas, or consider their suggestions runs the risk of being seen by others as insensitive, aloof, and arrogant." (James M. Kouzes and Barry Z. Posner, *The Leadership Challenge*, p. 180)

Think of the last few disagreements you've had with your partner. Really think about them, don't just remember that there was one last weekend. What was it about? Who did what and who was upset? What did he or she say, and what did you say? Did either of you walk away? Consider your behavior only in light of the quotes above. Were you listening to and interacting with your partner with respect? How would you have felt if someone else behaved with you as you behaved with your partner? Continuing to keep these statements in mind, replay the disagreements in your mind if you had responded with respect. Would you have behaved differently in a disagreement with your boss? A coworker?

This is not an easy exercise, we know. Stick with it, however. Don't get distracted by thinking, even to yourself, "Well, if she wouldn't . . ." or "Everytime he does that . . ." This is your time to evaluate your attitude of respect (or its absence) for your partner.

3. **Unique Technique.** Make a list of things you've accomplished, things you know how to do, and things you've done that not everybody else has done. Don't add anything into the exercise,

like listing things you've accomplished that no one else has or that you know how to do better than anyone else. This isn't a comparison exercise. For example, you may have raised children who are contributing members of society. Perhaps you bought a box of watercolors and taught yourself to paint. You might have always enjoyed singing, but finally took singing lessons and tried out for a part in a local theater production. Other people have done these things, too. The point is, you did them, and you feel a sense of accomplishment about what you've done.

Choose three or four things on your list that you are most proud of and that you think you deserve respect for. Now, did you receive respect for those things? Really think about this. If the person you most want respect from—your spouse or your dad or your big brother—didn't show respect for those things, look at other people in your life. Did anyone respect you for your accomplishments? If not, what are some of the reasons? In general, do you think you get the respect you deserve? Again, if not, what are some of the reasons? Did you tell anybody what you did? (Don't laugh—it happens all the time. "Well, no, I never told him I skydived. But he should still respect me for it.")

This part is a little more difficult. Think about how your partner relates to you in terms of respect. Think of him or her as merely a mirror of your own thoughts and feelings about yourself. Don't stop at just thinking, "She doesn't treat me with respect when she walks away while I'm talking." Look beyond her behavior to what you were doing or saying just before she walked away. How were you doing or saying it? Were you behaving like someone who is worthy of respect? Were you being respectful?

Anytime you look at yourself as if you are the cause of your life and its circumstances, it can be difficult. If everything is wonderful, it's easy to say, "Hey, yeah, I'm responsible for all this." When it's not so great, this isn't a fun exercise. However, if you make it a practice to look at people around you as mirrors now and then—as if you are the only one there and everybody else is a reflection—then you gain an extraordinarily powerful tool for your own self-guided growth. Please note, however, that we are not saying you actually are the cause of everything. Just pretend like you are periodically.

13 You Are My Best Friend

How many times have you heard someone say with great pride, "We have a wonderful relationship. You know, Matt is my *best friend*." It's particularly refreshing when that moniker of best friend is applied to a marriage, for then you have the sense of two people who have made it their goal to make sure that their partner is the best friend they have.

Our relationship is like that, and it means that there are no problems, no secrets, no victories, no defeats that are so staggering that they can't be shared. That's what best friends are for. When you graduated past the high school stage of cliques, clubs, and cattiness, you sorted out the people with whom you spent most of your high school years. These people fell into two categories: friends and acquaintances, and your best friend.

Many times, you hear mothers and daughters share the secret that they are best friends. You don't hear fathers and sons share that secret that often, even if sons grow up to be golfing and tennis partners or hunting and fishing partners.

149

Jack's twin daughters make no bones about the fact that they are best friends. Other twin siblings consistently report that also. It's the same with those brothers and sisters who are not twins, but you may find it much harder to have a best friend among siblings when there are many of you.

Best-friend siblings remain best friends if they make the effort to maintain the friendship after heading out on their own. A familiar saying is, "to get a letter, send a letter" (or phone call). Too often it seems that brothers and sisters make little or no effort to stay in touch after they have scattered to make homes of their own.

It's a shame, because that same lack of effort applies to partners in a relationship. When "Reach Out and Touch Someone" was adopted to increase long-distance telephone usage, the public picked up on the idea. It's very common to hear the phrase used between spouses, lovers, parents and children, and friends.

When Your Partner Is Your Best Friend

The thing about having your best friend be your partner is the opportunity for personal growth and relationship growth. When you trust your best friend, you put your life in that person's hands. That can be very powerful: "I believe so strongly in our friendship that I literally entrust things to you that I share with no other person."

It also signals that there is more to your relationship than the usual bonds of physical attraction. There is something mystical and spiritual in the relationship because only best friends would share information that could perhaps be detrimental or hurtful.

There are two ways we can see the above sharing of potentially damaging information working. Suppose you see your best friend's husband in an obviously intimate situation with someone not his wife, your best friend. Do you tell your best friend? Do you risk being labeled and "slayed" as the bearer of bad news? How do you say it if your answer is, "Yes. I know this person. Eventually my sharing this information will result in a better life for him or her. And that really is more important to me than whatever else we do together."

The other scenario is that you share something of a personal nature that could be potentially damaging if commonly known. Some possible examples of this type of scenario include:

"I had an affair with my last boss and broke it off. That's the real reason I had to leave my job."

"I was drinking on the job, and that's why they let me go."

"I so appreciate that you're trying to fix my brother up with a wonderful girl. But I need to tell you—my brother is gay. We don't discuss it in our family, and it's difficult for me to discuss it with you."

Rings, pendants, necklaces, bracelets, and other tokens that have been designed to represent friendship attest to the popularity of the idea. Friendship is valued more than romance in many relationships, strange as that may seem. How many times do you hear someone remark about the close friendship they have maintained with a brother or a sister, sometimes to the annoyance and exclusion of a partner?

We often do not have a choice of friends. Sometimes they are thrust on us in strange, mysterious ways. In the 1993 movie, *Fearless*, starring Jeff Bridges, a young boy becomes obsessively attached to Bridges because he was rescued by Bridges from an airplane crash. Bridges' own young son is jealous and hurt because this stranger latches on to his father with a fierce friendship that is threatening.

We often hear in couples' therapy sessions how annoying it is that one person in the couple will spend hours on the phone with a sibling and "won't spend five minutes talking to me." When confronted about this behavior, the offending party will say, "But my sister is my best friend."

The obvious question in such a situation is, "Why isn't your partner your best friend?" Too many times the answer is, "I don't trust my mate enough to be my best friend."

When Your Partner Isn't Your Best Friend

That's a tragic statement, isn't it? Of course, you have been with and known a family member like a brother or sister perhaps much longer than your partner. Yet there seems to be a lack of growth between partners if the best-friend status isn't shifting.

The strongest relationships are those in which the trust element is so complete that you want your partner to assume the title of best friend. Too often, however, the best friend is someone outside the relationship; someone that you can bitch to about the relationship. This is bad for two reasons. First, you put a strain on the outside friendship by burdening it with the intimacies of your relationship. Second, the person to whom you should be airing your complaints and with whom you should be seeking solutions is your partner.

If friendship cannot be a cornerstone, a key block in the foundation of your relationship, the relationship will lack a dimension. We think that a great deal of recharging takes place in that dimension. It is the dimension in which intimacy grows, and it involves seeing your partner in the added role of friend— hopefully, best friend. After all, you trust that you can tell your best friend anything and he or she will still be your friend.

If you need someone to talk to about life's problems you're facing, what is happening in the relationship that prevents your partner from being your best friend? This is like the question posed about an affair. An affair is never the issue, only a symptom of what is happening or not happening in the relationship to allow the affair to start in the first place. You may disagree with our train of thought, but we ask you to take a really hard look at your friendship status and fill in the missing pieces.

When you discover what keeps your partner from being your best friend, then you will have an important clue about what else is missing. This is the reason that recharging is so vital for the health and life expectancy of your relationship.

Friendship does not ask much in return. It asks only that you be there for your friend and that your friends will be there for you. When you consider what makes you give so freely that commitment to someone outside your relationship, you have to wonder what keeps you from offering it to your partner.

We are not naive. Everyone has secrets, some of them very dark indeed. You take a risk in losing your partner if divulge those secrets. Yet, how much better would you feel knowing that it was okay for you to be so vulnerable in your relationship? You are asked to arm yourself on a daily basis just to get through life with your partner. So what is the problem with allowing the vulnerability of friendship to be present? We'll tell you.

Your old nemesis, insecurity, jumps up on the stage of your life and takes over the leading role. You reason that if your deepest, darkest secret were to fall into the "enemy" hands of your partner, that secret would be all that's needed to destroy the relationship. You absolutely fail the test of trusting the process of love. You expect the worst.

Let's be frank. You may have every right to expect the worst based on past experiences with other relationships. Once again, however, we are talking about recharging your present relationship so your partner can be the best friend in your life. That simply isn't going to happen unless the two of you change whatever you have been doing to prevent that special friendship from happening.

What Makes a Friend?

We talk freely about man's best friend, the dog. What makes that so? Take a look at it. Your dog always trusts you, for one thing. As we have said before in this book, the love of your dog is unconditional. No matter how you treat him, he continues to love you without compromise. If you are lonely and depressed, a wag of a tail—no matter if it's a short stub of a pet bull or the long mane of a golden retriever—means just about the world to you.

When you need a friend, your dog is there as if to say, "Come on, snap out of it! Let's throw the ball or get you out for a badly needed walk. Then everything will be okay!" When you come home tired and miserable from the day's battles to a nose nudging at your hand for an ear rub, you know that you are needed and loved.

The dog asks nothing except to be allowed to be your friend. Try that on your partner and see what the results are. Let's just imagine that you ask absolutely nothing of your partner except to be your best friend. You won't ask for money, shared chores, sex, even tenderness. All you will ask is that he or she be your best friend. Do you think you could get such an unequivocal response?

Of course, it really isn't practical to expect that kind of thing. You are in a relationship for many payoffs for both of you, including friendship. What we are talking about in friendship here is the kind of sit-on-the-bed-and-let-it-all-hang-out kind of thing. You don't have to engage in the school-girl giggles or the crude-boy confabs of your youth, but you can look at the kind of friendship those years nurtured for you.

Was there really anything better than swapping heroic tales with the guys, even if there were some embellishments? Didn't dishing the gossip with that special girlfriend of yours provide just about the best rainy-day occupation? Well, return to those golden days of yesteryear and try it on for size again. What would really happen if you suggested to your partner that the two of you just share like best friends?

Would you get a "What the hell does that mean?" kind of reply? Or would you just get a look of bewilderment like maybe you've lost it? On the other hand, what if you explained that you really want to establish a friendship with your partner? You want a friendship that you have not trusted having before, and what would his or her thoughts be to that?

See, risk, again. You may have gathered by now that we don't hesitate to ask you to take risks in this recharging process. These are not risks that we have not asked ourselves to take, let us assure you. The rewards far outweigh the chances we take. A partner who is a best friend also is nonjudgmental. He or she is willing to follow the rules of listening without trying to make it better.

A partner-friend doesn't become parental or try to bully your feelings. He or she lets you cry without shame, and may offer you the comfort of enfolding arms or of knowing they are there in the same room if you want them.

There is something particularly intimate about having your partner as your best friend. It's as if the secure feelings never go away. The emotional garbage bags never have to get filled to over-flowing because you have someone—your best friend—who is there just to listen.

Making your partner your best friend does not mean you cut all ties from those special female or male friends. It's obvious that you and your girlfriend might really enjoy the sale madness at the local malls considerably more than your male partner would. The same goes for the poker party that may be an exclusively male thing (tradition and all that).

What we are suggesting is that when it comes to sharing on the most personal level your hopes and dreams, your failures and disappointments, it is wonderful if that sharing partner is your best friend. Friendship transcends so many barriers that we automatically have in our daily lives.

Friends Versus Best Friends

You certainly treat your supervisor or coworkers differently from the way you treat your friends. While you may have friends at work, they are different kinds of friends. Many conversations will be bitch sessions about work. That's a pretty natural subject. Gossip will run rampant with office friends, as will lunches that primarily are all centered around office politics, procedures, or rumor mills and more gossip.

When you lunch with your boss, you are careful about what you say. When you are the boss and you have employees with you, you probably rarely share much of what's going on in your personal life. It just isn't appropriate. If you have a business partner, the chance of being extra close friends probably isn't that great. In a small business, you each need a break from each other and gravitate to different circles for your more intimate friendships.

While you may golf or play tennis with office friends, you may picnic and bike ride with intimate friends. Activities that tend to be more private in their setting also tend to foster the kind of trust and sharing that empower intimate friendships. These are areas we would like you to look at when you examine friendship as a basic tool for recharging your relationship.

Friendship with your partner is a prelude to many things. There's better love, better sex, better planning, and better sharing of the future and burdens of the present when your mate is also your friend. If sickness strikes or if terminal illness presents itself in your lives, you will want your best friend to be there with you and for you.

When terror of the future may grip you with icy fingers, you'll want to be with your relationship partner, your best friend. At such times, the comfort level rises right up to the top of the scale. You somehow feel safer and more secure. The demons of fear subside. Now that's friendship.

Work as hard as you can to interview your partner for the position of best friend. What are the qualities you are looking for? What are the things that are missing when you look over the application? How do you feel when you share something very special with your partner as if he or she were already your best friend? These are all things that can be challenging to you and to your recharging efforts. Without a solid, warm friendship from your partner, your relationship misses part of the nurturing cycle it needs to grow and be bountiful.

Passion Points

1. **How Do You Spell F-R-I-E-N-D?** Think about friends you've had and have now. As you think about the following questions, jot down your responses and other thoughts about best-friend-

ship. We'll be working off this exercise in the later Passion
Points for this chapter. Do this exercise on your own. Start
examining yourself when you are in the role of friend.

- How did you meet?
- What was the evolution of your friendship—what hap-
pened after you first met that turned you into friends?
- What distinguished your best friend from regular friends?
- Are you still best friends? Regular friends?
- Are you in touch at all? If not, how did the friendship end?
- Who do you call with really great or really terrible news?
- Are you fairly certain that person will be there for you, or
does someone else come to mind?
- How did you nurture the relationship with your best
friend?
- What does he or she do to nurture the relationship?
- What motivated you to become best friends?

2. **More Spelling F-R-I-E-N-D-S.** Think about any patterns you
might see in your notes from exercise one. Keep adding to
those notes.
- Did you meet and develop friendships under similar circumstances? For example, maybe you were friends with
the group that invited you to sit with them during your first
day at lunch in a new school, and one of them became your
best friend. Later you became friends with a group during
particularly rigorous class and one of that group became
your best friend.
- Is the common factor acceptance? Kindness?
- What made you remain friends with the group?
- What was special about the person who became your best
friend?
- Were friends always from school, or did you also have
friends from hobbies, other activities, or sports?
- What is different about friendships with co-workers com-

pared to social friendships?

3. **You've Got a Friend.** Now, think specifically about your partner. Are you best friends? If you are, address the following questions from the idea of making your friendship even deeper. If you're not, then consider how you might develop a best-friendship with your partner.

    • With your mate, recreate the circumstances under which you've developed other important friendships. (For example, if you usually found friends in school, seminars, or classes, can the two of you find a class to take together?)

    • With your partner, how could you consciously follow similar steps that you went through when you developed friendships?

    • Can you visualize being best friends, or better friends, with your partner?

    • What thoughts, feelings, emotions, or resistance do you have when you think about being best or better friends with your mate?

    Write down some specific activities you can begin to nurture a deep friendship with your partner. What risk do you take by initiating those activities? What benefits can you see if you are successful?

4. **Something in Common.** Think about common qualities of your best friends through the years. What qualities did they have that distinguished them from other friends?

    Now ask yourself two important questions, and keep these questions open as you go about your daily routine; don't come up with an answer and forget about them. Let deeper layers of awareness unfold as you continue asking your questions.

    • Do you offer those same qualities of friendship to your

partner?
- Do you offer those same qualities of friendship to yourself?

14 Let's Not Be Judgmental

The tragedy of the 1994 murders of Nicole Simpson and her friend, Ronald Goldman, galvanized America. So did the subsequent arrest, release, chase and imprisonment of exhusband and superstar O.J. Simpson.

Everyone, it seemed, formed an opinion. Everyone read or heard something that no one else appeared to have seen or known. Americans were polarized around the burning question, "Did he do it or not?" How could understanding have been a keener part of this drama that *Time* magazine termed "An American Tragedy?" Even *Time* itself played a controversial role in the story by portraying O.J. in an artist's conception of the official police photograph of the defendant.

It was like a cascading river. Just when the water seemed smooth and negotiable, we approached another set of rapids and plummeted down a rushing torrent of misunderstanding and misinformation.

It seemed as if everyone had formed an opinion. So many people sympathized with the families of Nicole Simpson and Ron Goldman. Still others weren't able to let go of the sympathetic feelings they held for their superstar hero, a man who had become such a role model in the lives of anyone who ever watched him play football, saw a Hertz commercial, or enjoyed an O.J. analysis from the sidelines or studio.

Over and over, we Americans asked ourselves to be more understanding, to find some way to excuse even the bloody deed. It was as if we wanted it to turn out differently, that we couldn't bear to think that our hero could orphan two small children and paralyze a nation with disbelief. We were ready to grant understanding in its purest, most unadulterated form. So what happens that we can't offer the same kind of olive branch to the person with whom we are intimately involved in a relationship?

Take a Different Approach

Often, gaining a new understanding with another person involves simply looking at a misunderstanding in a new way. Jack had a most dramatic (for him) example of this during the summer of 1994. As always, Jack and the family golden retriever, Murphy, were out in the Cherry Creek State Park Wilderness Area just a few blocks from our home.

This is a morning ritual for the two of them, no matter what the weather or the season. We had discovered a nest with two baby horned owls and spent time watching them grow as the mother hovered around. One day, during the excitement of viewing the owls, Jack whipped out a pair of binoculars, and a lens caps flipped into the heavy underbrush, apparently gone forever. However, Jack kept looking for the cap, thinking that the snow would mash the underbrush and the lens cap would gravitate to the surface.

Each day, Jack and Murphy retraced their familiar paths in the park. Each day Jack would search the area where he had lost the lens cap, to no avail.

Then, this excursion into understanding happened. On an early Sunday morning in late June, Jack and Murphy entered the same general "owl" area, but from the opposite direction.

When they reached the owl tree, Jack reached for the capless binoculars to see if he could find the babies (now named Hansel and Gretel) or the parents. As he approached the spot where he had lost the lens cap months before, he looked down on the path. The missing cap was lying in the underbrush.

Jack felt like lightning bolts of comprehension had struck. "I was always looking for that damned lost lens cap by retracing the exact way we had come when I lost it. This morning, we approached from the opposite end and I spotted the lens cap immediately! It hadn't moved, of course. It was just that I had suddenly taken a new path to looking for it."

The story is long, but the point is well made. The missing lens cap was hidden from view (misunderstanding) when Jack kept looking for it the same old way on the same approach path. Viewed from this angle, the underbrush kept the lens cap hidden from his view. However, approaching the path (problem) from a different way led to finding (understanding) the missing cap that was there all the time.

Relationships breed misunderstanding simply because you have two people presenting conflicting points of view. Recharging your relationship calls for you to take a new look at the way you see a misunderstanding and then find a new approach to the problem. A new approach can produce a new understanding of the situation and, consequently, of your partner's point of view. This means that you are well on the way to reserving judgement on a particular issue presented by your partner until you have approached that point of view from perhaps several different directions. For example, when a woman asks her partner, "How do you like my haircut?" any man worth his life is going to answer, "Just great."

Affirmation and Understanding

She wouldn't have asked your opinion unless she wanted affirmation of her choice of hairstyle. If she didn't like it, she wouldn't have asked you in the first place. When couples develop the habit of reserving judgement until all the available facts are in and than making a decision based on those facts, understanding will take on a whole new meaning.

When a young boy says to a parent, "I don't understand that," what is the child really saying? Is he really telling the parent that his brain's synapses aren't firing in the right order and that is making comprehension impossible? Is he saying that something is not available in his realm of knowledge and therefore he doesn't understand? Or, like grown folks, does he mean he doesn't know what's making you behave the way you are?

In other words, "Mommy, I don't understand."

In your relationship, then, there may be the possibility that your partner's behavior eludes your understanding. So, it stands to reason that what you want to do as a recharging person is to find new ways to examine your partner's behavior. This will help you reach a new level of understanding that is not judgmental or, at least, not as judgmental as in the past.

It's very much like walking the path from the opposite end to discover the object which appeared hidden but suddenly appeared when viewed from a different angle. When you are short of patience and understanding with your partner, then you need to examine how his or her behavior drives you nuts. "It makes me crazy!" is a plaintive cry we hear from other couples with whom we discuss recharging.

When pressed for a more specific answer, one of the partners (the one being made crazy) will mention something behavioral that the other partner does. For example, Jane says, "When Harry starts channel surfing it just drives me crazy." What she's saying, of course, is that her partner's constant flipping channels with the TV remote wand (a behavior) is causing her to lose patience. Hence, we hear the followup comment, "I just don't understand why (there's the forbidden word again) he can't settle in and watch one program with me all the way through."

Jane confuses Harry's behaviors with understanding his reasons for doing things. She loses patience with his behavior and is judgmental in the process. In recharging, what Jane needs to do is look at the ways she can try to understand what makes her partner so restless during his relaxation time, TV watching with her.

We would suggest that Jane and Harry spend ten to fifteen minutes decompressing from the activities of the day before settling in to watch TV together. Harry obviously needs a chance to unwind. He may even need, God forbid, to talk with Jane about his day and hear about her day. It would be nice if Harry would realize that Jane needs some decompression time of her own, some time for herself to unload the cares of her work day. Harry must try to understand this need as well.

Understanding between couples, then, is also a realization of what must be done to help meet each other's needs. Therefore, in the recharging process the couple steps back a few paces and says, (before shooting off at the lip), "What do I need to see about this picture (situation), before I can get a complete understanding of what is needed to change it?"

So your loved one comes through the door loaded for bear and chewing at everything that gets in his or her way. It's very difficult to have much patient understanding for this kind of behavior unless you also try to understand what is causing the behavior. In order to understand what is causing the behavior, you will have to risk confronting the behavior.

"Gee," you harmlessly say, "it looks like you had a very rough day." Now the risky part: "Want to talk about it?" Assuming that you have made it this far without loss of life or limb, you can prepare yourself for one of two answers.

"Hell, no, I don't want to talk about it. Just leave me alone." Or, "Just give me a couple of minutes. I need to decompress."

If you have struck out with answer number one, then you counter by saying, "I can and will leave you alone if you want, but I will not be responsible for your bad mood or difficult day. Let me know when you're ready to unload your bad-day stuff." This definitely promotes growth in the relationship, sets limits as to what you will tolerate, and generates understanding between the two of you. That understanding is born of knowledge of the situation and offering solutions to the problems. Before recharging, a couple would probably just throw off a "to hell with you" remark and spend unnecessary time sulking.

Remember that all of recharging involves your willingness to change, to try doing things differently from before in order to make something new in the way you and your partner react in your relationship. Understanding is born of making decisions about what is happening or not happening based on facts you gather about what your partner presents.

It is impossible for you to be nonjudgmental if you simply respond to the behavior presented at the moment. Gather facts and sort the information presented as well as the information that is not presented by your partner. Keep asking the question, "What's wrong with this picture?"

Understanding means that you have sent and received messages in an appropriate and orderly manner. When Jack sees couples in marital or relationship therapy, he is never surprised to hear how each of the partners interrupt each other. Your ability to listen, to gather all the information that will keep you nonjudgmental, will lead to understanding your partner better than ever before.

If you realize that a large part of having a complete love affair with your partner lives in your ability to understand each other, then you are well on your way to an important key in the recharging process. Instead of wailing, "She just doesn't understand me," you can present behaviors that will make it very easy for both of you to understand each other and then to act in a positive manner on the problem.

Keep reminding yourself that it's not so complicated. After all, you are dealing with only three basic areas of life: love, work, and play. That's all there is; there isn't any more. When you understand that all life's problems fall into one of these basic categories, then it doesn't seem so overpowering, does it?

The process of understanding your partner means that you strive to turn to the same channel he or she uses to transmit information to you. It's like transporting yourself through the cosmic black hole to get to a new universe of comprehension with your partner. Remember the little kid saying, "You don't understand me" is really saying, "You're not hearing what I'm saying, feeling, responding to, or acting out."

Try to make understanding your partner a new experience based on information gathered to gain new fuel cells for the recharging process. You will find yourself losing the expression, "You just don't understand me," and replacing it with, "Thanks for giving me the information (tools) that helps me understand exactly how you are feeling."

Passion Points

1. **Grip Strengtheners.** Exercising and improving your ability to "get a grip" on your emotional reactions and understand your partner better can be a true challenge sometimes. Usually the times it is most important for you to be understanding is when your partner is experiencing an emotional response to something, and that usually triggers your own natural reactions. So you are required to do two things: to remain detached from your own automatic responses, and to try to put yourself in your partner's position. Either one of these is challenging enough on its own.

   Further, really understanding someone else means suspending all your judgements, evaluations, and interpretations. You have to put yourself in your partner's shoes to understand what he or she feels, not what you would feel in his or her position.

To help develop your ability to empathize with your partner, or to keep that ability sharpened, think of a recent situation in which you failed to be understanding. This can be a recurring situation or a new one that leaves you with the thought, "I simply don't understand what's going on with him (or her)."

Take the time to write out what your partner feels in that situation. Knowing your partner's background, personality, and strengths and weaknesses, what do you believe leads to his or her particular reaction or behavior? What's possibly behind what you see about his or her behavior? This is not what you think but what possibly can be generating your partner's responses.

For example, Eric and Marsha fight a lot about money. Fred thinks that Marsha doesn't understand the value of money. They have a comfortable income, but not a lot of money to spend on nonessentials. They have a joint account, both work as teachers, and Eric usually manages the account and allowances. When Marsha has some spending money, Eric thinks she spends it frivolously and usually has to ask for more money within a week or two of payday.

Eric feels frustrated by their inability to resolve the money issues and wants to do something about the frequent battles. As he writes down what he think goes on with Marsha, he continually has to set aside his assumption that she doesn't understand money. He thinks about how important her needlework is to her. She makes beautiful needlepoint gifts for friends and family and has even sold a few items at church bazaars. When he thinks back over what Marsha usually brings home from the shopping sprees he has considered frivolous, he realizes she purchases yarns and supplies for her hobby. Occasionally she'll buy some makeup, a piece of clothing on sale, or some perfume. Overall, though, most of her purchases end up being gifts or something for their home.

Eric also thinks about how important Marsha's craft is to her emotionally. She picks up her needlepoint when she's upset, she works on it while watching television or waiting for appointments. It's her form of basketweaving for mental health. As he thinks about this, he realizes that her hobby probably serves a purpose much like his running every morning. He just doesn't feel okay with himself when he misses his daily run. Maybe Marsha's spending isn't an indication that she doesn't understand the value of money at all. It may just be something she feels is necessary for her sanity.

The value of this exercise is not that Eric is necessarily right in his interpretation even after he's considered alternatives. The value is that he managed to break apart his belief about Marsha and suspend judgement long enough to see that he could be limiting his understanding of her behavior. The next time the subject comes up, Eric has the ability to understand what Marsha says to him about her need for more money, or what she spent her allowance on. He doesn't have to agree. He may need to ask her to do something differently, such as estimate the cost of supplies for a project so they can allow for it in the budget. The value is in the ability of the two to now proactively negotiate rather than react emotionally.

So take the time to consider your chosen situation completely from your partner's point of view. You can do this alone, so there is no loss of face for you as you give up your position long enough to reevaluate.

2. **Killer Presses.** For one week, resolve not to ask questions, evaluate, advise, or interpret during conversations of which you are a part or an observer. Simply listen attentively. Watch for nonverbal messages from your partner or participants in an exchange you're observing. Notice what emotions you feel during the discussion.

Moods and emotions are highly contagious. Think about how you feel shortly after your partner comes home frustrated and angry, or happy and fulfilled. Do you usually begin to feel the same way soon after, or do you unconsciously try to bring him or her around to your mood? Checking in with your own feelings can give you a clue about what others are feeling, although not necessarily for the same reasons. An important part of understanding includes recognizing feelings as well as content.

You will probably fail to perform this exercise all the time during the week. Sometimes it will be inappropriate. If you have a client or a customer, naturally you'll have to ask some questions. However, at least try to consider the exercise during all exchanges during the week you choose.

If possible, do this exercise during the same week as your partner, and share what it was like for you at the end of the week. Take turns, as during a Ten Minute Drill.

3. **The Second Part of Understanding Is to Be Understood.** It may seem unfair that you are assuming responsibility for both understanding and making yourself understood, but the benefits are well worth the effort.

Someone once said, "The essence of communication is intention." In seeking to be understood, first be clear that your intention is to be understood—not to win, put down, or embarrass your partner. In keeping with your intention, consider your partner's thinking style. Perhaps you are a linear thinker, laying things out in logical steps and progression. Your partner, however, thinks holistically, considering the big picture and trusting that the steps to the desired outcome will take care of themselves. Both styles are valuable, but require different approaches to a goal. You may need to describe what you see as the goal first so your partner understands. If you're the holistic thinker, you may need to struggle with outlining the steps to the goal you visualize so your partner can understand.

In this exercise, too, writing down what you want to have understood is extremely valuable, particularly if it's something important to you. You can organize your thoughts, consider your partner's thinking style, practice bridging any gap there might be between your styles. Then when you do discuss the issue, you can be more responsive to the questions your partner asks—they will clue you in to what you need to further clarify to be understood.

15 Togetherness: Relationships Need It

Does a relationship, particularly a recharging one, need togetherness? We believe the answer needs to be hedged. If Cyn were to give the definitive answer she would say, "It's just as important to be apart sometimes."

Jack, on the other hand, would say, "The more a couple is together, the more they tend to stay together." Who is right? Both of us.

When you look at the status of couples today in this busy society, the idea of much togetherness might be impossible. Day care centers are not a luxury, but a necessity. Both partners in most relationships work. We are often with other professional couples. When we ask what is going on with them, they usually reply, "We don't know, we haven't seen each other much!"

In our own schedules as you already know, we work at different levels of productivity. Jack writes in the early morning hours or at least before noon, while Cyn writes only after *The Late Show* or *Saturday Night Live*. That might be a bit exaggerated, but you get the idea. Cyn=owl, Jack=lark. So where is the togetherness factor in the relationship?

The Quality of a Relationship

We have learned not to worry about when we'll spend time together but what we will do with the time. A recharging couple needs to make quality time the format for whenever they are together. Plus, it is important that a couple spend time apart. It is in being apart sometimes that you gain the necessary elements to recharge the relationship when you are back together.

You probably have seen those couples we call "velcro couples." These are the people who seemed joined at the hip. They can't move without one another. They can't afford to be apart for ten minutes, much less ten days. They are constantly hanging onto each other as if to make some spectacular show about their love and commitment to one another.

You get to the point where you would like to find some way to pry them apart, only to find out that they like it that way. How many times have you wanted to be with a sister, a son or daughter, or all by yourself? However, the fear of hurting your partner prevents you from taking time away from each other, even to spend an hour or so alone with your relative, your friend, or, heaven forbid, yourself.

Look at it this way. The quality of your relationship is measured by what you can contribute to the relationship. We talk about it a lot, asking ourselves, "What can we bring to the table to increase the value of our time together?" In this regard, we treat ourselves a lot like labor and management.

We sit down and begin to "put things on the table" as if we were drawing up a contract. Cyn might say, "I'd like to go roller blading." Jack might say, "Let's go for a bike ride." Jack then rides his bike along the path on which Cyn roller blades. He maintains a very safe distance from her in case she wipes out. We are still spending quality time together, but both of us enjoy doing what we wanted to do. We have, therefore, successfully negotiated some quality time for our period of togetherness.

But we also need time to ourselves, and so do you. It is impossible even for the velcro couples to spend every waking minute together. You must have individual experiences in your daily lives so that you have something new to contribute to the relationship.

Think of all the times you eagerly wait to hear from your partner about what transpired during his or her day. You want to know what new experiences she had, what thoughts and feelings he had while you've been apart.

Bringing those new experiences into the relationship is like striking the flint to recharge the fire in your relationship. How dull and boring would it be if neither of you could ever report anything that was new?

Has your relationship felt a lot like that? Have you thought that the solution was to spend more time or even some time together? Well, the feeling you may be having is absolutely correct. You are feeling as if your relationship is slipping away from you, or has already slipped so far into the abyss that it will be impossible to retrieve it. Not so. What you need is to reevaluate how togetherness is achieved and what you do with the time involved.

Planning Your Togetherness

So, we come to the importance of planning your togetherness. How much time of each day or week should you spend in each other's company? How much time do you need to be alone? How much time is comfortable for you to spend in each other's company? These questions may seem absurd in the light of being a couple. It is just naturally assumed that a couple will spend time together. That's the reason you became a couple.

Planning time together if you have small children is even more of a challenge than it is for couples with no children or older children. Your choices are more limited. We've devoted an entire chapter to this subject, but for now—to help start you thinking about how you can plan time alone—here are a couple of ideas.

You can spend some time alone after the kids are in bed—to talk, work on some of the exercises we've included in the Passion Points, or to make love. The major point is to spend time on yourselves, not to deal with day-to-day mundane matters. You must have some time to stay in touch with each other emotionally and intimately, or all other aspects of your life together will begin to suffer.

If you can afford a babysitter periodically, or have a family member or older child who can watch the younger children, take advantage of the opportunity occasionally to have a night out. Spending money is not necessary, if money is a consideration. Walk the mall and window shop, go to a crafts bazaar and sketch ideas for your own projects, go to a discount movie, or visit the art museum. Take a drive and watch the sun set (maybe even make out in the car).

The recharging process demands that you be healthy as an individual and are able to stand on your own two feet and get out of the needy category that you may have adopted as your general way of life. If you cannot be strong as an individual—free, independent, and capable of pulling your own weight—then it stands to reason that you won't have much to contribute to the relationship.

Therefore, we believe that togetherness can be reinforced from a sense of oneness. This means that it's okay for you to be alone for periods of time without your partner. Is it okay for you to take a mini vacation alone? You bet. What would make anyone think that you don't need the opportunity to do a little self-recharging so you can handle the bigger chore of recharging your relationship?

It's good for you as a couple to spend a couple of days on your own. If you are worried that the relationship won't stand a short, separate vacation, then your relationship may be in trouble. It is nice for togetherness when each of you has a weekend to be alone. Sometimes it's good not to have to worry about anyone else. It may be nice to eat when and if you want, or to get up or sleep in without raining on the parade of your partner. Some uninterrupted time alone, away from your usual responsibilities, can be invaluable for thinking, planning, untangling the threads of your life.

When you do spend time together after being apart, you have so much more to give to one another. Sharing life experiences that happen to us when we are alone is one of the blessings of being in a relationship. You can talk to your partner, infusing him or her with what you have seen, heard, read, or experienced while apart.

Look at how your dog treats you when you arrive home after being gone all day. The animal nearly wags its tail off, greeting you as if you had been gone for weeks, even though it has been only hours since you were together. Isn't this a much different reaction from the one you get when you have spent the whole Saturday at home in the company of your pet? He or she hardly notices when you make a short run to the video store or go out to mow the front yard.

The animal is with you during your time at home, experiencing togetherness. When you come home after hours of absence, however, your pet is anxious to greet you, to give you the opportunity to share ear scratches and tummy rubs. In effect, you and the animal recharge your relationship with each other every day you are apart for long hours at a time.

Togetherness as a Treat

If you and your human partner are never apart and are committed to spending every minute of every hour together, then instead of recharging your relationship you are probably burning it out. Looking at togetherness as a treat instead of a demand is what recharging is all about.

Cyn and Jack practice what we call "hanging out time." About once a month, one of us has some mundane chores that need to be done or that we want to do. These are chores that are particular in nature to our individual interests. Cyn wants to run to the craft shops for supplies and ideas. Jack needs to make lumber-yard and hardware runs. Together we like a particular hardware store visit just to see new stuff and gadgets.

In order to be together for quality time, we plan to "hang out." If Jack needs to be at the lumber yard and Cyn doesn't have any particular errands, Jack might be invite her to come with him just to hang out together. When Cyn is going mall crawling, she invites Jack to just come along for "hang out" time. It's fun. We do it, and yet don't feel as if we are crowding the space of the other person. We also reserve the right to decline "hang out" time. That's okay, too. So is the occasional choice not to invite the other person because of "secret stuff"—gift shopping, for example. But the invitation is always extended at least once a month. For us, it means that one of us has to be willing to stop what we are doing and devote some "hang out" time. It's amazing how refreshing that can be.

You can do the same thing by approaching how you spend your time together in a different fashion. Togetherness also means windows of opportunity for talk, for sharing. The couple that will make it a routine to take an evening walk together will always tell us that this is when they do their best talking. There is magic to having a different setting when you want togetherness.

Going for a drive seems to be a lost art these days, particularly when gasoline prices are very high and considering the pressure to reduce unnecessary driving because of pollution and other environmental concerns. But driving somewhere out of town is purposeful. If you were planning to eat out, what's wrong with going to a neighboring town or community to try one of their restaurants?

The Adventure of Togetherness

The fact is, recharging couples should try to make an adventure out of their togetherness. We are fortunate to live in the Denver area, where the mountain communities are very close— within a 30- to 45-minutes drive. A short drive to the foothills for breakfast can be as recharging as an expensive flight to another city, although that is certainly part of our particular togetherness plan.

When you go to museums, art galleries, or exhibits, you can feel very secure in splitting up for awhile just to satisfy your personal interests. Bookstores are a good example of this. It's okay to go to bookstores and explore the stacks on your own, enjoying the wonderful delights of satisfying your own personal reading and browsing tastes.

What joy we find in going to the other partner and showing him or her a particular treasure of a book, sharing what makes its subject interesting and meaningful to you. When we are in Santa Fe, Cyn invariably makes a beeline for the rock and mineral shops. She could spend hours browsing their many geological treasures. Jack might leave her there to look for Kachina.

We have done these things separately, but they are an expression of togetherness because they are shared times that represent quality to us. Togetherness should not be seen as a prison sentence. It should not be an albatross around your neck, for either of you. Look at togetherness as a privilege of being in the relationship. In other words, you are together not because you have to be, but because you want to be and because you have something to offer one another in that togetherness.

Working Together

What about people who work together—partners who operate businesses together or practice law, medicine, run stores and teach in the same schools? For them, togetherness can very easily turn into a dirty word. Often we hear the complaint that these people never get away from each other.

Sometimes that's true. But here are a few ways that a recharging couple who must work together in a business or professional life can function better. First, it's necessary to imagine that you have two doors in your life and two keys to those doors. When you both are ready to leave your business, you turn the key in that door and lock it for the day or the night. No more business talk, okay? At the same time, you open the door to your personal life as partners together.

This works for you even if you don't have the responsibility to physically lock up your place of employment. We're talking about "locking your doors" emotionally. In your mind and your heart, you are done with the business for the day. No talking about it, and no overtime.

The other thing that we find essential for recharging couples is to be bold and take separate cars to work occasionally. We know that this is not very economical and that you can probably find more good reasons to keep on carpooling, but you can have an entirely different perspective about your relationship if you at least arrive at different times. The couple who eats breakfast every morning, gets in the same car to drive to the same workplace, eats lunch together, has their afternoon break together, and then rides home together to spend time together is "togethered" to death.

It may start off being romantic, this much togetherness, but it gets old in a hurry. Some part of that routine has to be broken up with time alone. You need a place for you to recharge yourself away from your partner so that when you are together, you will have something fresh to contribute to the relationship. We have been practicing something that is so simple in its freshness.

Reversing Partners

When you are out with another couple, instead of sitting next to your partner, try sitting at the side of your male or female friend, across from your partner. It is amazing how the flow of conversation changes, and how refreshing this simple adjustment in seating changes the course of relaxed, friendly talk. This little experiment forces you to do something that isn't very easy if you are seated right beside your partner. It forces you to look at your partner from across the table, drawing him or her into the conversation and more readily including the other two people.

Dinner hostesses have been doing this for centuries, of course, but only recently has it become a very "in" thing for four people to split up like this in a restaurant booth or a poolside beach table. Picnic tables are ideal for this arrangement. It is totally nonthreatening and yet intriguing. You are together yet you are also with a new partner. Your conversations tend to be much more inclusive, and no one really ever feels left out.

When we ride bikes, play tennis, or play bridge with our friends, our skill level is a lot less embarrassing if our life partner is our game partner. Nevertheless, we try to split up—Cyn partnering with a male friend, Jack with a female friend. Thus, while we are together, we are also in friendly competition. We don't have to hide our individual skills (or lack thereof) for the sake of our life partner. It is a recharging tool that offers fun and laughter, even after we have left our friends and can rehash the game of cards or an athletic event.

Keep in mind that the essence of the word *together* could be taken to mean two gathering, and that's exactly what the recharging couple wants to do. Both of you gather individual experiences of your daily lives and share them with one another as special times. Togetherness takes on new, fresh, and meaningful colors for your life as a couple.

Passion Points

1. **Hang Out at Your Hangouts.** Pick a weekend or other day to hang out together. Do things together that you don't usually do. Eric and Marsha (from the Chapter 14 Passion Points) did this exercise and learned some new things about each other. Eric went with Marsha to her yarn shop and watched as she selected items for a gift project. She did what he asked and gave him an estimate for the project, so he was prepared for the expenditure. He was impressed by the way she compared prices and quality of the materials for the project. He had never dreamed

there were so many yarns and threads and designs for needle-work. Not only did Marsha buy all the materials she needed for less than her estimate, but Eric found a number of ideas for gifts for her.

Marsha then went with Eric to buy a new pair of running shoes. He told her about some of the things that were important in a good pair of shoes and what he wanted and why. She hadn't realized he'd been running in a pair of shoes with holes in the soles, nor did she realize that there were shoes for just about every kind of sport and athletic activity imaginable. They both developed a deeper appreciation for the other.

Be sure to do this exercise willingly. Don't agree to spend time with your partner and then complain the whole time. Bite your tongue if you have to. You might find you actually enjoy doing some things you never thought you would.

2. **All by Myself.** On another weekend, spend a day apart from each other. If you have kids, pets, or another responsibility that requires one of you to be home, take turns having a day away from the house. Your assignment is to do anything, but do it without your partner. Go out with a sense of adventure. What happens that you can share with your partner when you return? If you simply want to go to the library to read, how do you feel when you're finished? What did you think about? Did you have any insights about yourself or some problem you've been having? How did you feel about being alone?

We often meet for breakfast, then go our separate ways with an agreement to meet at home in the late afternoon. Or, we'll do our separate activities and meet for an early movie and dinner out. This way, we have a time to reconnect and share what happened for each of us during the day.

16 Kindness: How to Give, How to Get

W e're not getting mushy on you. Rather, we're leading you to understand that these last chapters have been dealing with emotions and their expression. The feelings you have for one another and the manner in which you express them is what recharging is all about.

How long has it been since you even thought about the importance of these qualities we have been writing about? Maybe never? Then what would make you believe that we could help you recharge your relationship without giving consideration to kindness? It isn't something you can measure in doses. It isn't part of the "new age" wedding or union ceremonies, unless one of the partners believes kindness to be next to faithfulness.

Be Considerate

Kindness, in relationship terms, is the ability to be considerate and responsive to for the person with whom you share your life.

Consideration ranks as the most important element of the act we call kindness. "He is so kind to me," recalls one woman we know. For Jo, that meant her husband didn't bang her around like the first one did.

"She is kind to my children," says the proud husband and father of three children by a previous marriage. "She always corrects their manners, but in a way they like." Is this person expressing kindness or consideration for the way people would like to be treated? Is kindness calling your partner's mother more frequently than he or she does, or just a matter of being politically correct?

Kindness, we believe, is a lot like receiving mail. To get a letter, you must first write a letter. To get kindness, you must first give kindness. In a recharging relationship, kindness sometimes can be walking a very thin but distinct line. You might be doing a great favor, and hence are very kind, to tell your partner that a cavalier attitude with the checkbook will lead to big trouble.

On the other hand, you risk being verbally blown away by being parental with such a suggestion. You might be expressing kindness when you suggest that a partner's color sense in clothing is not the best. You save them much embarrassment from making poor choices in clothes.

This hits merrily home for us. Jack is constantly kidded about needing to have "Granimals" sewn in his clothes to make sure the shirt he has chosen will match the color of the pants he will wear. On the other hand, when he chooses clothes for Cyn, they are remarkable for their taste and perfect colors for her without ever a return to the store of purchase.

Kindness takes many turns in a recharging relationship. It is one thing that makes hugs and kisses without sex so important. A warm embrace or reassuring hug speaks volumes about kindness— an almost gentle persuasion that is part of the recharging couple's complete plan. It is kind to suggest that your partner visit regularly with far away relatives by telephone or in person. This is kindness not only to the relative but also to the partner in your life.

When you express this kindness to one person, you touch many. Thus, in the Bible, Christ exhorts in so many words: "When you show kindness to one person you also show it to me." Getting kindness for yourself may be another matter requiring more skill. You know people who are the epitome of kindness to everyone else yet can't seem to even buy an ounce for themselves.

It makes you appreciate the old philosophy that tells you that if you take in a stray dog off the street, feed it, pet it, and are kind and gentle to it, you are the first person he will bite. Sometimes it seems that you simply do not inspire one bit of kindness from your partner. Maybe it's time that you asked for kindness as a means of recharging your relationship.

If you ask for what you want in a relationship, the odds are far better that you will get what you ask for. This eliminates the requirement for your partner to second-guess your needs. First, however, you must define what kindness means to you.

Defining Kindness

For some people, kindness would be not saying harsh and ugly things about your partner's family. Perhaps kindness might mean offering to do a particular chore that you hate to do. One person's definition of kindness will seldom be the same as another's, including your partner's. If you go to the root word of kindness, the singular word kind, which means child in German, could suggest that all actions toward your partner are childlike or framed in the context of innocence, as expressed by a child.

Gentle, childlike behavior is often interpreted as kindness. Kindness in a recharging relationship is, in effect, the absence of controlling and selfish behaviors. In short, we come back to kindness being synonymous with consideration. If you can invoke consideration from your partner, then the chances are great that you will also receive kindness.

As we have said, only you can detail what kindness means for you. Once determined, then you are able to see to it that you practice the behaviors that mark you as being kind. It also sets the stage for you to receive kindness from your partner.

We know a couple whose definition of kindness means that he watches the children one day a week so she can have a day off. We frankly don't consider that as kindness as much as simply sharing the normal load of parenting—something he should do and without treating it as a great gift from him. But it isn't important what we think, because to her, he is expressing a great kindness. When defining kindness for you and your relationship, it is only important that you and your partner become aware of the need for expressions of kindness, of consideration. If Jack scrapes the snow off Cyn's car, it is an act of kindness, consideration, and love. If Cyn parks her car so Jack can manage to get his in the garage, we would probably not rank that as an act of kindness. However, if Jack finds a little love note on the top of his day planner in the morning, he definitely considers it an act of kindness as well as love. It's all in the eyes of the beholder.

Apologies for wrongdoings and harsh words are acts of kindness, no matter what other definitions you have. When there is closure of unhappiness between two people, that is kindness. That is consideration. Offering an apology is an expression of sorrow that harsh words were spoken. It also says that you would rather be at peace with your partner—in a warm and comforting environment.

Thus, you are expressing kindness. Gentleness is also more than a reasonable component of kindness. Kindness, gentleness, and consideration make for sound recharging. The eloquent writers of all ages have often referred to a "kind and gentle man," or her "kind eyes also spoke of gentleness." Gentleness and kindness go together like Ben and Jerry of ice cream fame. It's hard to imagine one without the other.

Take Another Look

The recharging process calls for you to take another look at the person with whom you are in a relationship. How long has it been since you really recognized that this person is a living creature with feelings, which are subject to wear, tear, and brittleness? When you trample on those feelings, you are not recharging. Rather, you are charging headlong into a war of frayed nerves and hurtful behaviors hurled back at you with a velocity and venom that would put modern weaponry to shame.

Kindness is being aware of your partner's feelings and the knowing that, to some extent, you are the chosen protector of those feelings. In every way, both of your feelings are on the line, exposed, tender, and vulnerable. Only kindness and acute (short-term) awareness, coupled with chronic (long-term) gentleness can protect them.

The recharging couple is clear that kindness to each other is not a reward for helplessness. That philosophy is demeaning to the quality of the relationship. The kindness rendered to an elderly person who is physically disadvantaged is considerably different from the kindness you show to your life partner.

The kindness expressed in donations to the homeless, work for an earthquake relief fund, or work for the AIDS coalition is a kindness of humanity. It's something that a person does as a responsible member of the human race. The kindness one shows to a partner in a recharging relationship is a vehicle for advancing the momentum of the relationship.

Jack's grandmother used to tell him, "You catch a lot more bears with honey than with vinegar." This wasn't an original adage with her, but the point has stuck. Kindness in itself can be a wondrous method by which you share love in unseen ways. However, you know that the partner who is kind also is the partner who is gentle, considerate, and aware of your needs and feelings—in short, a partner expressing love for you through the kindness at play in the relationship.

Kindness in a recharging relationship is bringing the chicken soup and French bread on a tray to your sickly partner suffering from the flu. Kindness is offering a back rub for aching muscles or lending a helping hand for mundane chores that have become temporarily overwhelming. Kindness in a recharging mode means having a travel pack of tissues handy for the weepy parts in a movie.

Kindness is the consideration you show when you have her bike tires pumped up before you start the ride, or lay out a favorite shirt for him to wear because you like how he looks in it. Kindness in the recharging relationship is not doing the little things you know drive your partner nuts.

Kindness is throwing bread crumbs onto the deep winter snows for the ducks and the birds to eat. It is also being the one to suggest that you prepare dinner because you know your partner had a particularly rough day. Kindness is not bitching when asked to pick up something at the store that your partner wants. It is asking if there's something you can pick up at the store while you're there.

In short, then, kindness is a reciprocal exchange. You and your partner exchange consideration and acceptance of warmth, love, and helpfulness. Such exchanges make your lives more complete and more fully charged with the spirit of being a couple.

Passion Points

1. **A Kind of Writing.** Take the time to think about, and preferably write down, what kindness means to you. Remember some times people have been kind to you. What did they do? How did you feel? Has your definition of kindness changed over the years? What have you done that you consider kind?

    Share your definition with your partner. Talk about your experiences of kindness with each other.

2. **Killing Doldrums with Kindness.** With your partner's definition of kindness in mind, do something every day for at least one week that your partner—not you—will think as kind.

3. **Two Kinds are Better Than One.** As a couple, be kind to someone you don't know well or at all. Sometimes we think that a kindness that takes us out of our way or involves some personal sacrifice counts more on some mystical kindness scoreboard. But consider the act of letting a merging driver onto the freeway in front of you during rush hour. (We sometimes entertain ourselves by considering the ripple effect throughout the universe of all drivers performing this kindness, even if only during one single rush-hour period.) This can even become a meaningful sacrifice if you let someone go in front of you who is clearly a jerk.

4. **My Kind of Day.** At least once a week, preferably more often, do something kind for yourself. Just determining what this act might be could prove challenging in itself. It could be as simple as forgiving yourself for a little mistake you would usually beat yourself up over.

17 Sex: Use It or Lose It

Oh sure. And you thought we would never get to the subject of sex. We can hear our readers now.

"They talk about everything but sex as a means of recharging a relationship."

"Isn't sex important in the recharging process?"

"They simply want us to talk about things but never do anything."

Well, here it is. There is a very good reason that we chose to treat it last. We believe, and we practice, that without all the other sixteen basic recharging subjects you have read in this book, sex won't mean very much. How's that again? Simple, really. If a couple is not practicing forgiving and forgetting, not caring or communicating, not making a commitment or sharing and trusting, then how can they possibly be having great sex?

We aren't comfortable with you just having sex or even good

sex. We are talking dynamite, no-holds-barred, recharging sex—that can only be happening regularly when all the other elements are in place in the relationship.

Making It Happen

Good sex doesn't just happen. We make it happen. When a relationship is steeped in the elements of recharging, then a couple is wrapping themselves in intimacy. When you and your partner have intimacy, you are on the road to great sex.

What we are suggesting for the recharging couple is a look at how to reach your sexual potential. This is something that most people never do. People in their 40s, 50s and 60s are often the most sexually responsive to one another. They are not limited by the conventional wisdom that as one gets older one loses sexual interest. When couples lose sexual interest in each other, it's not so much a matter of age as of expectations.

Seventeen-year-old boys can have instant erections, but this has very little to do with an attractive partner. They can get the same erection from seeing panties on a store mannequin. As people get older, they need more stimulation. Sex can become boring just because a couple is doing the same old thing.

Recharging couples have to throw off more than their clothes. They also must throw off the old attitudes and beliefs that have kept their relationship in the holding pattern of boredom for much too long. While it is true that men may reach their genital sexual prime in adolescence, this does not mean that it's all downhill from there. Unless, of course, you simply want to continue to be a statistics expert in a relationship.

Are You a Statistic?

Statistics experts want to measure how long it takes a man to have an erection, how long it takes to have a second erection and, of course, the strength of ejaculations. The statisticians in a relationship will always focus on genital responsiveness. Statisticians overlook changing how partners perceive themselves sexually and the risk they take to change.

Sexologist Dr. David Schnarch, writing in a 1994 issue of *Psychology Today*, talks about the flow pattern of good sex:

"Sex is a lot like Zen archery. The preparation to shoot the arrow is arduous. Shooting the arrow is easy. Once you do the hard work of personal development, all you do is let the arrow go. The arrow shoots itself. Sex flows."

We encourage you to prepare to "shoot the arrow," because we believe in the process of discovery and experimentation as a means of recharging. Masters and Johnson have taught us that sex is a learned skill. The problem is that most couples have proven to be pretty poor learners. They simply repeat the same old things that they have done from the beginning of their relationship. Or they continue to avoid things they never even tried because it was too messy, scary, or some other reason.

Jack teaches a course in Sex and Sobriety to other therapists in workshops throughout Colorado. He refers often to the need for therapists to help clients with sexual "stubbornness" to overcome what is often called "terminal prissiness." Terminal prissiness is an attitude that sex is just too messy and "unclean" for some people to try to experiment.

Trading in Old Attitudes

We encourage you to throw away those old attitudes and be willing to open the doors to new excitement, particularly to the idea of game playing with your partner. Since our childhood days, game playing has been a big part of the growing process. We have used games to learn to ride bikes safely, to drive cars or fly planes, and to invest in or buy real estate.

Whatever stage in our lives, games have been a method we have used to learn, teach, and gain more enjoyment from daily living. It's the same with sex games we play with our chosen partner. We first ask the questions:

1. What do I like in the way of sex play?
2. What don't I like? Do I know the reason?
3. How about frequency?
4. Who needs to initiate our sex?

In an uncharged relationship, you may not have enough energy to care whether sex happens, much less who initiates it. Think of it this way. When you first got together, there probably was a heat of passion that engulfed your times together. You didn't pay much attention to who started what. It just happened, perhaps quite frequently.

As you settled into your relationship and sex became something routine and mundane that you generally took for granted, what would ever make you think that your sex life would continue unabated in its ardor? Remember when we talked of the need to treat your relationship like a living, growing plant? How it required attention, nurturing, and to be treated as if it were a third entity in your lives?

The Changing Scene

Your sexual relationship calls for that same kind of treatment. So you feel like it's all downhill and there aren't many or any surprises in the bedroom anymore. Well, there's one of the problems right there. Maybe you should move your sexual activity out of the bedroom and onto or into:

1. The front seat or back seat of the car
2. The living room floor
3. The kitchen table
4. The den
5. The basement
6. The garage, in one of the cars
7. The bathtub or shower stall
8. The guest bedroom
9. The favorite recliner
10. The office (his and/or hers)

Well, you get the idea. There's practically no place where you can't initiate sexual activity with a little planning and the right time of day. How interesting it would be for you to move the entire scenario of your sex life as if the two of you were just meeting for the first time. Ask yourselves, "How imaginative would we be then?"

In our short list above, we didn't even get to the really fun places—like the swimming pool, the beach, the ocean, on a sailboat, in a railroad pullman bedroom, in a sleeping bag camping out. What can we say, except, use your imagination!

We always suggest to couples that they treat each other like they were trying to win one another again. Cyn has a saying that goes something like this: "If you want to make love to someone, you'd better treat her (him) like somebody you want to make love to." Treating your partner like a lover increases your chances of getting a lover's response.

How often have you bitched at and complained about one another for most of a day, then felt disappointment because love making fell short of your expectations? Wonder why? To get a lover, be a lover. Using your imagination and moving your love action from the traditional bedroom into a different arena can do wonders for recharging.

This is part of the game playing. The fantasy scenes that you create with one another belong exclusively with you. You are the writers, the actors, and the directors in whatever love drama you care to create. We have a hotel in the Denver area that caters to fantasies. At this place you can pick a theme such as Old West, Jungle, or Roman Bath.

We have heard of these places in several cities, and they are all pretty much the same. You select a theme room which is decorated as you would expect. Rooms are equipped with hot tubs, waterfalls, the works. Honeymoon theme rooms have heart-shaped beds, satin sheets, and all the trimmings. These places cater to the game player in all of us and to the idea of having fun in your romance.

Having Fun Again

You do this game playing or fantasizing in other areas of your life. What's preventing you from doing it in your sex life? We went to a delightful restaurant in Ft. Lauderdale called "The Caves." Each table was set in an alcove and decorated to create the feeling of being in a prehistoric cave—all quite intimate, clever, and mood provoking. Menus were on "stone" tablets presented by "caveper-sons" dressed appropriately.

Theme parks are making billions of dollars, attracting millions of people. When party-goers wonder what to do to raise money for a charity, there is always a theme, a fantasy brought to life to help open the pocketbooks. Look at Halloween. How about the holidays of Christmas, New Years, and Hannuka? We play at almost every other part of our daily lives, but somehow believe our sex lives should be conformist, stable, and maybe even dull and boring.

Well, let's get over that! Acting out fantasies means you both become very vulnerable. That's one of the reasons that "character" roles work so well in sex. You can be someone else. When playing the character of a pirate, a cowboy, a dance-hall stripper, or a comic book hero, you can lose many inhibitions that might have limited your dull sex life.

Vera is a lawyer married to Jim, and she also is a mother. She maintains a certain decorum most of the time. She found, however, that her occasional sex character role of Mazie the dance-hall girl allowed her to be pretty uninhibited. She bought a tape of *How to Strip for Your Husband and* practiced. Talk about a recharging relationship. Vera told us that things had "never been better" sexually between the two of them since they began to play in their sex lives.

There is enormous pressure on couples these days just to keep a relationship together. The August 15, 1994 issue of *Time* devoted the cover and a major portion of the issue to the question of whether infidelity is "in our genes."

Whether or not you agree with this, we hope you at least con-sider that man's (and woman's) natural impulse toward restlessness with one mate can be stemmed if there is a sense of adventure in the relationship. Just think of all the reasons you had for wanting to be in this relationship in the first place. Have they all disappeared with time? Is there no longer any sense of the excitement, passion, and desire for playfulness that might have been like powerful magnets between the two of you in the beginning? If the answers are in the negative column, then you have absolutely nothing to lose by trying something new.

If your relationship has forced either of you to use outside stimuli such as pornographic videos, books, or pictures, then try making your own videos or picture album. How wonderful to see your mate getting turned on watching yourselves, rather than strangers, as the stars.

Just think how you would feel if your partner made a grab at you after being turned on by watching sexual encounters of two complete strangers on a video or pictured in a magazine. We doubt that you have felt very validated as to your own physical or even personality charms after such stimuli. The experiment for the recharging couple is to have fun photographing and videotaping yourselves. Enjoy the pleasures of yourselves in one of the most wonderful and rewarding aspects of your lives, the act of being sensual and sexual with each other.

Strangers and Other Lovers

Making love with a stranger is one of the most common of all fantasies. Every time that you and your partner can play at the "stranger" game, the more fun and worthwhile it can be. Have you thought of meeting in a restaurant or club as if the two of you did not know one another?

What would it take to call your partner and play a little by pretending that someone gave you his or her number and "Would he or she be available for a movie or lunch?" You could arrange to meet at a special place. Describe what you will be wearing and ask for a description of the person, the "stranger," you are meeting.

Please don't treat this as adolescent silliness. Playing works because it stimulates the imagination. The most vicious enemy in a relationship is taking your partner and your relationship for granted. When two people just assume that their sex life is going to be boring, then that's how it is. If a couple looks to what could make it better, it automatically begins a roll toward being better because the participants' attitudes are the spark that starts the recharging.

There is a piece of "psychobabble" called "stable attributional style." It means the belief that things (sex) have always been boring or dull, it is boring and dull now, and it's always going to be boring and dull. Your job, as a qualifying recharger, is to make that stable style unstable in a major way. It is up to you to take a step back from the relationship and say, "Hey, wait a minute! What's wrong with this picture (of our sex life) anyway?" When you take the necessary and calculated inventory of what's missing, then the chances for correction are really much better. Here's one example of where the old adage, "If it ain't broke, don't fix it," doesn't apply. You should assume that your sex life (uncharged) is broken, and you will damn well fix it (recharge).

The really great thing about recharging the sexual part of your relationship is that it helps you initiate the intimacy portion of your life that has probably suffered the most. Face it, if the two of you cannot treat each other with care, trust, and respect, and if you can't treat your partner as your very best friend, then you are missing intimacy. If you are missing intimacy, then it only stands to follow that you will not be engaging in great sex, and in fact may not be having much sex at all.

It is the tenderness, the loving friendship and understanding of one another, that sets the stage for fulfilling sex, particularly recharged sex, to happen. Wanting to wear a special outfit or taking a moment to apply fresh lipstick or a splash of favorite aftershave does more than just stimulate the flow of testosterone and estrogen. It speaks more loudly to promoting the sense of warmth and strength, the desire to be held and to snuggle or to give a massage, even if there will be no sex right at that moment. A couple may begin to anticipate the touch of one another again, even though it may have been years since the newness was there. They may feel the miracle of each other's bodies, the caress of gentle hands and tender lips. Then they are truly into the recharging process.

Breaking Boundaries

Experiment and imagine! Break your boundaries so that there is an open field in which to play with your partner again. By playing, put into your sexuality the very elements that make you unique to one another. Practice the Passion Points and write new ones for yourselves, realizing that the only limitations in the recharging process are the limits that you set for yourselves.

Dead cells cannot be recharged. Live but neglected cells, which simply need attention and the jolt of new life and spirit, can not only spring back to life but also surge forward for many years to come. In doing so, they recharge with a new and lively spirit and determination.

Passion Points

1. **Fun With Exercise.** It seems that it's impossible anymore to pick up a book about anything that doesn't mention diet and exercise. We're no different. We won't deal with your blood pressure, your cholesterol, your drinking or drugging, your weight, and all that stuff. We'll just talk about diet, exercise, and sex.

   The exercise has two parts. The first is to begin noticing how you feel after you eat different foods. Notice, of course, physical reactions that might indicate allergies or intolerances to certain foods. More pertinent, however, is to notice how you feel emotionally, mentally, and physically. Do some foods make you feel lethargic, sleepy, or sick? Do you ever eat anything that makes you feel energized and alert? What about how you feel after big meals, small meals, vegetarian meals, or main-dish salads? Do you notice that any foods make you feel sexy? If so, is it a feeling associated with a memory or do you think it's the food itself? Do you care?

The second part of the exercise is to start stretching. Try to stretch every chance you get, but at least several times during the day. Definitely try to stretch before getting out of bed in the morning and before going to bed at night. If you have ever watched a cat stretch, use it as an example of how this should be done. Stick those arms way up over your head and imagine you're trying to touch something just out of your reach (every-body's had to do that sometime). When you're sitting, clasp your hands way over your head and push them up, then back as you bend your entire torso into an arch. Then bring your body and arms upright again, and lean way to the front, pressing your hands in front as far as you can, when standing, bend forward and try to touch the floor. Bounce once to try to get just a little bit closer. If you can touch the floor, try touching the floor about a foot in front of your feet, then about a foot behind your feet. If you can touch the floor easily, then you probably already know all about stretching. Don't hurt yourself with any of this. Concentrate on stretching out the kinks and knots and feeling your muscles doing something besides tensing up. This isn't a workout to make you sore.

Now, what's the point? After you've noticed what foods make you feel good and which don't, then try to eat the foods that make you feel good before engaging in lovemaking. Eat light-ly. Sex actually is exercise, and you can be pretty uncomfort-able if you've just eaten a big meal. The same is true if your diet includes a lot of foods that cause allergic symptoms. All we'll say about bloating, gas, sinus problems, and all those other symptoms is that in our experience they don't make one feel sexy. Also, allergies and chronic pain or discomfort of any kind sap your energy.

If you suspect that a prescription drug is causing side effects that may be affecting your sexual activity, please consult your physician.

The stretching is to help you loosen up, to feel yourself move sensuously, and to expand your range of movement during lovemaking. There are positions that can greatly enhance your sexual pleasure, but you have to be able to get your body into those positions to enjoy them. Obviously overall fitness, strength, and health are important, but stretching is something you can do anywhere, anytime, regardless of whether you engage in any other form of exercise. The exceptions, natural-ly, are if your physician tells you not to stretch or if you have a disability.

2. **Getting to Know You.** This is short because almost everyone reading this will resist it. Do the best you can to keep the fol-lowing in mind: You don't know as much as you think you do about sex. This isn't debate material; we don't really care how much you know. If you come to your partner a little bit hum-ble, you create a vast opening for sharing what works and does-n't work for both of you. You can learn wonderful things about your partner and yourself if you don't shut down possibilities for greater pleasure by assuming you know it all.

3. **Sexual Maintenance.** Write the following sentence and post it in a private place where you will see it often or commit it to memory: "My name is _____, and I am totally respon-sible for my own orgasm." (Credit for this goes to New York psychologists Bill and Marilyn Simon.)

Repeat this sentence to yourself frequently. See how many times you and your partner can say it to each other without laughing. Think about it. Substitute other words sometimes for "orgasm"—happiness, success, feelings, behavior, or whatever else comes to mind. Notice over time how your behavior changes during love making. Do you show or tell your partner more often what feels good? Do you find yourself doing a little research at the library to learn how to enhance or control your orgasms? Maybe you decide together to go to a qualified therapist with training in sex therapy for a "tuneup." Do you actually start doing some of those things you read about in magazines?

4. **Mad (?) Scientist.** Experiment, experiment, experiment. If you began doing the exercise we recommended in the Passion Points in an earlier chapter, you've been practicing getting comfortable with being uncomfortable. Anything new can be uncomfortable at first. If you don't like something at first, give it another chance. If you still don't like it, then don't do it anymore. There is one thing so simple that we forget it all the time: If something never changes, then it's always the same. That includes sex.

5. **Hooray for Hollywood.** We mentioned earlier what fun it can be to make a video of yourselves making love. If you haven't done this, then do it at least once. You can rent video cameras for an evening if you don't own one or can't borrow one. For the purposes of this exercise, watch the video you make later and notice how you feel while you watch it. Also notice how you appear in the video. There are reasons videotaping is so frequently used in sales and public-speaking training. There simply aren't many better ways to see yourself the way others see you. Do you move? Do you ever smile? Do you ever pay attention to your partner's responses? Do you hate how you

look? Do you like how you look? Do the two of you look like you're having any fun? The more honest you are with yourself about what you see on the video, the more power you give yourself to improve your sex life. Your responses to the video tell you what you need to work on, want to work on, or are happy with. If you lay there like a stick during lovemaking, you may be feeling a lot but just haven't ever realized that you don't show it. Next time you have a choice. In truth, you'll probably like what you see more than what you think.

6. **Spread the Good News.** You've done a lot of hard work: we know, because we've been doing it, too. So this final assignment both of you must do every single day: Be passionate about your love affair with your partner. Make sure you spread the passion around all over the rest of your life. Make everyone around you crazy with curiosity about that little smile on your face and your aliveness. Just tell them you recharge everyday.

18 Kids: Recharge or Short-Circuit

"**H**ow," you may indignantly ask, "are we supposed to recharge our relationship, when we are very lucky indeed to even find time to see each other?" This sentence most often issuing from the harassed couple who are putting so much of their time and energy into parenting—a noble but very exhausting full time (it seems) and all encompassing occupation.

And you are right. We clearly understand that it is very hard to find time for each other; to find the opportunities to recharge a relationship, and to examine the relationship in detail, when most of your waking (and even sleeping) hours can be taken up with child rearing.

But that's the point. It would be easy for you and your partner to put every ounce of your strength and efforts into parenting and then you know what? There's very little time left to have a relationship, much less recharge the one you have. And we know that.

So, the problem is for you and your partner to admit that one of the things that may have sparked your relationship in the first place was the desire to have a family, but then you lost control.

Nurturing the Relationship

The pendulum has swung the other way and now perhaps you have invested almost all the time in parenting and no time at all in the building and nurturing of a relationship. Little kids .and "middle-age" kids require constant care. Do we even need to mention teenagers? But it doesn't matter. If we were to ask the same pointed question of you who are raising a family as we do of other couples we are trying to help recharge, what would your answers be? If we were to ask when the last time you had a real date with your partner, what would your answer be?

How would you respond to the questions about going out for dinner? About role playing to spark a lagging or nearly dead sex life? What about getting away for a night or a weekend alone? Too tough to even think about?

Well, that should give you some idea of how far you may have slipped in the caring of your relationship. With all the energy pouring into your children, there is hardly any time left for you and your partner to even think about the elements that we have been discussing in these previous chapters.

Centers of Affection

It is very important that you step back a couple of paces and take a look at the picture of your relationship since you had a family. One of the most significant changes that has happened is probably the subtle or maybe not so subtle shift in the centers of affection that exist between you and your partner.

Who still gets a good night kiss? Who wonders if he or she is still important to you? Not the children, we'll bet! Much of the outward shows of affection between two adults often get drastically curtailed or even eliminated when children come on the scene.

We have talked to many couples who have complained (in good natured humor of course) that "since little Sam or Sally came on the scene he/she doesn't waste much time on me!"

We say that they were "good natured" in their reply. Laughter is often an exchange medium for tears. In Jack's psychotherapy practice, he has dealt with many couples whose sex lives and plain old social lives were abandoned with the onset of parenting.

Guilty, Your Honors!

The problem, we find, is that a couple begins to feel downright guilty when they talk about taking a vacation without their kids. It's almost treason to assume that the parents could go to Las Vegas and not drag their kids who just might miss all the new family attractions of that city.

Or is it possible that a pre-Christmas trip to Rockerfeller Center and the delights of New York City could be taken by just the two of you without guilt? It's tough, but it can be done! You might even find that the reasons the two of you got together in the first place might come bounding back into your unconsciousness without the children along.

In a particular favorite comic strip, *Drabble,* drawn by Kevin Fagan, the mother and father of the family went off to Las Vegas, leaving their children at home. Mom spent all of her time calling home to check on the kids, every hour on the hour. The "kids" of course were Norman, a college student, left in charge of his precocious little brother who was perfectly capable of taking care of the whole family.

We get so used to wrapping our lives around our children that we allow, and invite guilt to be a partner when we think of doing something without the involvement of the children. However, in the recharging process, a couple will soon find that when they are recharging their relationship with each other, they are also recharging their relationship with their children. And this is a very important fact. Just as you have proven to yourself that an hour or so away from the normal routine of work, home, or other family obligations, often provides new strength, determination, and insight, so a little time away from your children also sparks a new appreciation for them and their role in your lives.

Give Your Kids Credit

Your kids will understand that you and your partner need time with each other if it looks like there is a payoff for them. It's really okay to tell your children that you and your partner "are going to have a date", for example. Of course, they will want to come along. Be patient and explain that just as they have special times to be with their friends, such as at school or day care, so do you have special times that you are with your best friend, who is your partner.

When some couples come to therapy sessions with Jack they bring their children. Once in a while this is allowed by Jack but not all the time, as children can be disruptive to the therapy process and may force the couple to focus on child care instead of on relationship problems.

However, on those occasions when the kids are in session, Jack is always amazed at how the children put great emphasis on what the office (his) is doing for the parents. One very bright youngster told Jack that she likes "coming to the Talking Center."

"What?" he said, not knowing where that name came from.

"Here," she replied, giving a wide sweep of her arms to Jack's spacious office. "This is the Talking Center because Mommy and Daddy started talking to each other after being here!" Pretty simple stuff, eh? Kids know the importance of parent communications, so what's the reason they should not be a part of the process of recharging?

Making Kids a Part of the Plan

We suggest that you let your children in on plans that will mean you and your partner will be gone one evening a week to have your weekly date (as strongly suggested to you earlier in this book!)

"Can't we go to the movies with you?" will come from big saucer wide eyes, set in pitiful upturned little heads. The answer is "No." "This is time that Mommy and Daddy plan to spend with each other," you say bravely, ignoring the little gurgle that is beginning to be heard from the waif's throat. "Just like we spend special time with you when we read you a bedtime story, or play with you at bath time. Mommy and Daddy need special time for play, too!"

Well, you can use your own imaginative dialog, but we were simply giving you a sample track on which to run when ignoring the tears and the pouty lips that mark the weaponry of your children. Be sure that you book a favorite sitter or relative on a regular basis to help the child have a sense of security and to know that the night out between you and your partner are so special that you plan for your children's pleasure too by having someone with them they really like.

We are not much in favor of spur-of-the-moment recharging when smaller children are involved. It's much better for them to be part of the routine of knowing that you have a set night out for the two of you. Obviously these nights or days away from your children will have to be augmented with other special times that require to be out without your kids. But as a general rule, the basic recharging will come with just you and your partner getting back to the basic dating routine we talked of earlier. By making your kids a part of the plans but not participants in the plan, you help them understand the importance of you and your partner's devotion to your relationship.

Let your kids help "select" what you are going to wear on your date. We put "select" in quotes because we surely don't think your children's choices of clothes would probably be appropriate, based on watching them play "dress up." However, what you can do is select what you are going to wear and then get the once over approval by saying, "Daddy will really be surprised that I'm going to wear this (dress, pants, jeans, what have you) because he likes it so much! Don't you think he will be pleased?"

Or, the men say, "See if my black shirt is hanging there in the closet, Shane . . . your mom likes that shirt a lot!" While we don't condone bribery of any kind as a part of recharging your relationship, we do find that bringing home a treat from the movie such as some of the box of candy you bought, assuming you can control your impulse to scarf the whole thing yourself!

Often, you can bring home part of the dessert from your dinner, or perhaps just a roll, croissant, or some such item. We knew a couple who made it a point to skip dessert at their meal and stop at an ice cream parlor and brought home bulk-packed ice cream occasionally and then made a mini-party of eating it with their children and the baby sitter. This was not done every time of course, but enough times so that the kids became coconspirators with their dad when he began talking about a night out with their mom.

The Power of Visible Affection

Recharging with children present involves a lot of visible affection, too. When is the last time you allowed your children to see the two of you kiss? We don't mean the compulsory peck on the cheek, we mean a real kiss, with arms around each other? What about holding hands? How long has it been since your children saw you watching TV with your arm around your partner's shoulder?

We're obviously not suggesting that the main event passion of your lives be shared with or in front of your children, but too often couples are simply too shy to let their children see any show of affection at all. How many times in therapy will the therapist hear "My family isn't one to give hugs or be affectionate?"

Couples will role model what they are used to, and it's up to you as a recharging couple to break that old tape and replace it with a new one! It's really an okay thing for you to hold hands or to exchange a loving embrace. Your children will instinctively know they are part of a secure and warm environment and they will demonstrate their affection more openly.

The same kinds of open affection should be demonstrated on them as a natural spin-off to their observance of the two most important people in their world demonstrating love and affection. The recharging couple will get caught up in the process of rejuvenating the relationship that may have been teetering and ready to fall since the children began consuming so much attention.

When the recharging process is really working, it has a wonderful side affect. Everyone in the family unit feels a sense of togetherness that may have been missing. When older children are involved, you will find that they will begin doing some things together again that they may have put off for a while. It is not uncommon in our experience to observe that teenage brothers and sisters will find time for the two of them to take in a movie once in a while and report back on what fun it was. All of this is sparked by observing the new recharging interest that their parents are practicing by dating again or by having TV-less meals once a week or more.

Family: The Basic Unit

Siblings forget that they once were the real source of each others play time and security. As they grew older and went into different friendship circles, they have lost touch with what being "family" is all about. The recharging couple helps point up the fact that our family is still the basic unit of love that should be nurtured so that it continues to be a rewarding place for us in times of difficulty and hardship and love, peace, and prosperity.

The recharging couple sets the pace for the rest of the family. And while you may think this is so basic and simple, let us tell you, there are visible signs that appear in your children when they see that their parents are making a new effort at rekindling a relationship. Do even small children sense when things are not okay between parents? Yes, they do. You know it well. It is just like a family pet who heads for the basement when voices are raised. The pet doesn't know what words are being said but it does understand that an argument is occurring and the peace and tranquility of the family unit is disturbed.

Children respond to the same kinds of changes in voice levels, moods, environmental changes such as shut or slammed doors or faces that are not smiling but frowned or tear stained. An interesting series of tests was run years ago by a group of child psychologists to test reactions to stimuli of newly born children. The experiment called for the mother or perhaps a nurse to lean down over the child and begin smiling, softly laughing and cooing and generally presenting a very happy picture for the baby to see.

The baby would break into a smile, gurgle and coo and be generally responsive to the human being dominating its scenery. Then, the experimenters moved the female out of the lone of vision and held a large white card with a painted "smiley face" on it, forcing the baby to look only at that.

No sounds were made, but the baby would look at the exaggerated smiling face and break into the same coos and gurgles as if it were the human face! The infant, it was concluded, was responding to the stimuli of the smiling face, whether human or drawn, as opposed to the fact that human nurturing was all that could be responsible for a feeling of well being and contentment.

Smiling faces on parents who are obviously recharging a relationship will be reflected in the faces of their children, even though the kids might be left at home with a sitter once a week. You, as parents, may not realize just how important it is that you take time for your relationship. You can get so caught up in the whole business of parenting that it's easy to forget you came together to be parents because of your love and commitment to one another. So what makes you think that your job to keep that love and commitment alive has ended when kids arrive?

There is a wonderful little single panel cartoon feature written and drawn by Gary Wise and Lance Aldrich, called *Real Life Adventures*. A recent panel showed a young couple seated at a restaurant table, menus lying before them, and both of them obviously out on a date. The husband is saying to his wife:

"Oh, her looks so nice." And she replies: "And so does him, yes him does."

The caption for the cartoon reads: "You can tell when parents of young children aren't getting out enough."

Isn't it the truth! The couple who is interested in recharging has simply got to risk breaking away on a regular basis to reclaim the romance, the reality, and the renewal of their basic relationship.

Passion Points

1. **Hit the Road Jack.** To emphasize a point made earlier in this chapter, plan at least once or twice a year to have an overnight time with just the two of you—without the kids. We realize this can be tough to do—especially without parents or other family members living in your area.

    Try some creative babysitting ideas. Trade off with another family, having your friends' kids stay over at your house when your friends go out of town. Maybe there are neighbors that would be willing to have your kids spend the night (provided your family all feels comfortable with them). The point is for you to get away.

2. **Don't Know Much about History.** To help your family see how recharging works, make a conscious effort at meals or family gatherings to talk about your first dates together and your more recent fun times recharging (the ones you can talk about in front of your family). Let your family hear and see that you are still having as much fun now as you did when you first met.